Stories of the Black and
Asian Migrant Pioneers

England
Our England

Gurnek Bains,
Bryony Heard
& Kylie Bains

Stories of the Black and
Asian Migrant Pioneers

England
Our England

PROFILE
EDITIONS

8   PREFACE

10 INTRODUCTION
    # WELCOME TO ENGLAND

14 CHAPTER ONE
    # ARRIVAL
    The Shock of the New
    Interviews with Yvonne Bailey-Smith, Swarn Kaur Bains, Mahesh Patel, Mae Milner-Brown

36 CHAPTER TWO
    # HARD LABOUR
    The Survival Grind
    Interviews with Mota Singh, Errol Turner, Swarn Kirpal, Shazardi Hashmi

58 CHAPTER THREE
    # CONNECTING WITH THE LOCALS
    Getting to Know You
    Interviews with Lucky Gordon, Kamala Sharma, Gloria Leslie, Kenneth Jean-Marie

86 CHAPTER FOUR
    # IDENTITY
    Finding Ourselves
    Interviews with Nic Careem, Piara Singh Bains, Elouise Edwards, Stefan Kalipha

108 CHAPTER FIVE

COMMUNITIES LOST AND FOUND

Connections in a Strange World

Interviews with Vijay Dhir, Darance Licorish, Mustapha Matura, Val Milner-Brown

140 CHAPTER SIX

WEEKENDS

The Lighter Side of Life

Interviews with Ralph Adu, Sheron Pearson, Satish and Maya Sehgal, 'Gus' Osmond Philip

162 CHAPTER SEVEN

BREAKING BARRIERS

Going Beyond Our Station

Interviews with Dharam Dass, Russell Henderson, Horace Ové, Louis Mahoney

182 CHAPTER EIGHT

PASSING THE BATON

It's Your Turn Now

Interviews with Deloris Smith, Jenni Francis, Derek Blake, Gina Matharu

196 HOW TO THROW A BLUES PARTY
198 HOW TO THROW A BIG FAT INDIAN WEDDING
200 AFTERWORD

204 INDEX

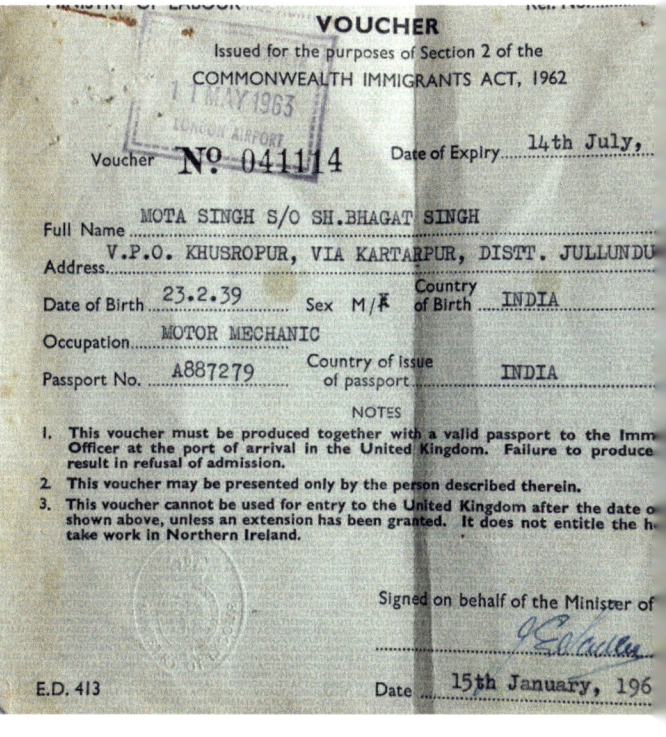

PREFACE

As children of the first-generation migrants to this country, we had always been fascinated by the stories that circled around us. But as we grew older and our parents passed into old age, we realised that these stories were gradually fading into oblivion.

We resolved to capture them, and the images that could bring them to life, before it was too late. From the moment that we thought of this project, many people pitched in to help us. The idea that we needed to capture the stories of this 'silent generation' of migrant pioneers before the memories disappeared forever resonated with people. Like us, they had heard the stories from their parents, grandparents, aunts and uncles and flicked through dusty photograph albums, but not seen any of this recorded in an easy and accessible form.

We slowly started collecting the material. It was a labour of love. We wanted stories from all walks of life – from people who had led ordinary lives, contributing to key areas quietly and without recognition, as well as those who had broken through in some way. We also wanted to create something that was accessible and would sit on a coffee table spurring conversations and interest. Above all we wanted to create something that could be handed down to our children so that they too could understand their backstories.

Over the years we collected a lot of material. We have tried to include as much of this as we can, but inevitably had to make some choices. We apologise to the people whose stories and images we were not able to include.

Furthermore, although most were comfortable going public, a small number of the contributors, while being happy for us to share their stories, wanted to remain anonymous. This was a generation in which many did not like a spotlight being shone on themselves, and we have respected their wishes.

We want to thank all the pioneers who gave us interviews and photographs. This book is about honouring your lives and we salute your dedication, resilience and dignity as you established a base from which your children could move onwards and upwards. This book is offered as an account of the varying experiences of those times but also a record of the age-old human tradition of moving, needing to settle and call a new place home.

Gurnek, Bryony and Kylie

INTRODUCTION

WELCOME TO ENGLAND

For many British people, ruling other people in far-off lands was seen as a romantic, exotic and somewhat quaint notion, but it was a different story when these people were on the doorstep, competing for their jobs.

Starting in the late 1950s, this country experienced an unparalleled wave of migration from Africa, the Caribbean and the Indian subcontinent. Self-evidently, this migration was transformational for the migrants themselves, but it also had a deep impact on this country, changing it in many obvious but also subtle ways. As our stories indicate, many of the migrants already felt a part of Britain and they came with hopes, fears, beliefs and myths about the country that they were entering. Psychologically, many were on the 'back foot', coming to rub shoulders with people who had ruled their countries for centuries. Seventy years after this mass migration, many members of this first generation of migrants are dying out.

As they pass, so their personal stories pass into history and oblivion. This is particularly true because this was a generation that focused on the practicalities of getting on with life rather than recording things or talking openly about their feelings.

The purpose of this book is to capture the experiences of this generation in a vivid, evocative and accessible manner. In part, this is simply an exercise in respecting and paying homage to people who made extraordinary sacrifices to cope with a swathe of challenges, for the most part in a stoical manner without complaint. We also want to capture these experiences so that the children and grandchildren of that generation appreciate what their forefathers have been through and understand their own backstories.

We share stories of those who broke through and 'made it' in many sections of British society, as well as those who formed the backbone of our NHS, the transport industry and other critical industries and services.

Although Britain has moved forward decisively to become a vibrant multicultural society, progress can never be taken for granted. The Covid-19 pandemic has hit BAME (Black, Asian and Minority Ethnic) communities much harder than others, illustrating the divisions that still exist. The Windrush scandal and the hostility to Eastern European migrants, illustrated by the Brexit debate, also show that prejudice and rejection of 'the other' are never far from the surface.

By bringing to life the contributions and the challenges, as well as the immense help and acceptance that many received from the host community, we hope that these stories will help to surface our better instincts when reacting to those who are trying now, or will try in the future, to make their home here – as countless generations have done before.

← A Caribbean man in a street in Soho, London, 1949.

→ Letter from the Home Office.

A landscape of remembering and recounting imbued with an inevitable nostalgia of passing time takes us through the immigrant's emotional and cultural journey in Britain. We present an intimate view and an homage to this generation's experiences, to ensure that future generations remain connected to their roots.

APPENDIX 1.

SIX POINTS WORTH REMEMBERING

ON ARRIVING IN BRITAIN

Make sure you know the full address of the place to which you are going to and KEEP IT HANDY.

2. IF you go into lodgings make sure you know what the rules of the house are (ask the Landlady) with regard to:-

    a) Meal times.
    b) What hour you are expected to be in at night.
    c) Convenient times for baths.
    d) Rules for inviting guests.

3. YOU will have to pay your fare to London as this is not covered either by your boat or air ticket. Fares are as follows:-

THIRD CLASS SINGLE

Plymouth to London	225 mls.	£1. 12. 8.
Liverpool " "	193 "	1. 8. 4.
Avonmouth " "	127¼ "	18. 7.
Southampton " "	79¼ "	11. 8.
Newhaven " "	56½ "	8. 4.
Tilbury " "	24 "	2. 9.

PROVINCIAL STATION		PASSENGERS ENTRAIN AT		FARE
Birmingham	110 mls.	Euston Stn.	London	£- 16. 3.
Liverpool	193 "	" "	"	1. 8. 4.
Wolverhampton	123 "	" "	"	1. 7. 2.
Coventry	94 "	" "	"	- 13. 9.
Nottingham	123 "	Kings Cross	"	- 18. 1.
Newcastle	268 "	" "	"	1. 19. 3.
Manchester	183 "	Euston Stn.	"	1. 6. 10.

PASSENGERS FOR WALES WILL LEAVE FROM PADDINGTON STN. (LONDON).

4. WHEN you arrive in London or anywhere else in the United Kingdom, having settled at an address, first register at your nearest Employment Exchange for employment. You will find this out by:-   a) Asking a Policeman,
                      " at the nearest Post Office,
                      consulting a Telephone Directory.

5. HAVING registered for employment, you will be well advised to make yourself known to the office of

    The Welfare Liaison Officer,
    Colonial Office,
    Sanctuary Buildings,
    Great Smith Street,
    London, S.W.1.

Either visit in person or telephone for an appointment to:-
Abbey 1266, Extension 633.

6. The Welfare Officer will be pleased to advise you on any matter in connection with employment, accommodation or personal problems.

February 1968: Asian immigrants from Kenya arriving at Heathrow Airport, London.

CHAPTER ONE

ARRIVAL

One can't go back. In changing places, you change. We live in relationship with where you are, through the eyes we have now, and mediated through the people we have become.

TAIYE SELASI, 2004
AUTHOR OF *GHANA MUST GO*

CHAPTER ONE

ARRIVAL

THE SHOCK OF THE NEW

The gripping chill was coupled with another unexpected reality: the almost eternal greyness of the English sky sat so strangely and low above them, giving their new world a washed-out, blurred existence. The contrast to the warmth and vibrancy of their homelands could not have been starker.

The prosperity and protective promise of the 'mother country' was a tantalising draw for many Asian, African and Caribbean people in the 1950s and 60s. For some, whose lives were dominated by hardship and poverty, it was a chance to ease that burden and begin a better, more fulfilling life. For others it was the opportunity to provide a strong education for their children and the potential for them to pass through the many doors it could open. Some didn't have a choice as they were being ejected from their home country; for others it was the sheer adventure that brought them here.

The nature and strength of immigrant motivation to leave their homeland was, and had to be, significant because the path to Britain was often not an easy one. To start with, the process of attaining passports was frequently riddled with bureaucracy, tedium and frustration, no doubt testing the stamina and resolve of even the most determined families. Then there was the journey itself to contemplate: How will we get there? What does it cost? Can we afford it? Can we all go together or does one of us have to go it alone first? How long will it take and what will we find when we arrive?

Budget travel was yet to hit the world and most immigrants came by sea, which was expensive. This was often tackled initially by a single member of the family, typically the father, going alone to Britain and working, sometimes for several years, to save enough money to bring his wife and children over. Alternatively, stowaways would brave the ocean journey hidden in the dark corners of a ship.

After much anticipation, the first moments of arrival were, for most people we talked to, eclipsed by the shock of the weather. Full-frontal, biting winds were something few had expected or prepared for. The cold seeped into their bones and stubbornly lingered. Some were fortunate enough to benefit from the forethought of charities that kindly provided second-hand winter coats to new, shivering immigrants. The challenge of dealing with their physical environment was often dwarfed, however, by the emotional strain. Desperate loneliness, homesickness, bewilderment and despair burdened many of these early pioneers, and we explore this further. Some were only children, coping on their own in a strange new land. Their loneliness was set against the backdrop of trying to carve out an existence in Britain, where the ways of attaining housing and employment were as unknown to them as the unwritten rules of social etiquette and how they were expected to behave. Perhaps most poignant is the fact that many bore these challenges in silence and with dignity.

Immigrants who were called to the UK were given little or no support from anyone and were left to make their way as best they could.

← April 1956: Part of a contingent of 1,000 West Indian immigrants with their luggage at Paddington Station, London.

The contrast in the level of support that immigrants and their families received was striking. Indeed, British people reacted to immigrants in very different ways. At one extreme there was generosity, kindness, warmth and a desire to help and embrace newcomers from the colonies. At the other extreme were stories of blatant racism, emotional abuse and an underlying distaste and anger towards immigrants. There was also a marked distinction in the way immigrants were treated by their fellow countrymen who had recently settled in Britain. Asians seemed to take newcomers in as family – often providing a place to stay, food and even money to send home.

Inevitably, part of the settling-in process involved looking for a place to live and for gainful employment, which often proved difficult. At a deeper level, searching for jobs and working in Britain raised issues for migrants about whether to dismiss, or adapt or retain their native culture. Rastafarian dreadlocks, Sikh turbans and traditional forms of dress were unusual additions to the streets of Britain in those days and employers weren't always comfortable with them. Many immigrants felt the pressure to conform and although some pragmatically shrugged their shoulders and did so, others steadfastly, and often bravely, held on to the symbols and customs of their own heritage.

Many British people at the time felt threatened and that recent migrants were competing for their jobs. Today, arguably, we see this reflected in the attitudes of British, as well as the Asian and Afro-Caribbean communities, towards Eastern European immigrants who are perceived to be taking their jobs and in the result of the 2016 referendum to leave the European Union to 'gain control of our borders'.

↑ Transferring cargo at the Pool of London, 1949.

↑ Dockers watch a steamship at Limehouse Cut, Lower Pool, the original port of London, 1949.

→ Colonial House hostel for newcomers to settle and find their feet. A group of immigrants from the colonies unpack their luggage in a shared room in a hostel, 1949.

You would have watchmen on the ship and we would sneak past them to get on the ship. You would hide in various places. At first you would get in the lifeboat and when you get clearance you go somewhere else – coal bunkers, hatches, fridges. Yes, a lot of us died in the fridge. LUCKY GORDON

YVONNE BAILEY-SMITH
PSYCHOTHERAPIST, ADVISOR FOR YOUNG MINDS AND MOTHER OF NOVELIST, ZADIE SMITH

After my grandmother died in 1968 in Jamaica I came to England to join my mother as at that time you were not allowed to live with a male parent.

My mum worked at St Bart's Hospital here; but in Jamaica she had been a seamstress and designer. It would have been so hard for her to build up her clientele again so she got a job as an auxiliary nurse. She came here when I was only seven years old in about 1961. By the time I came to England, I was a teenager and had lost the relationship with my mother and also somehow lost my relationship with my siblings. It was very tough settling here.

I know my mother experienced a huge amount of racism. She suffered indignity but did not talk about it, but I saw it with my own eyes. I saw it when I was young, a fellow nurse pushing her out of the way. I told that lady off – I was only young but would not stand for it! People like my mother paved the way, we stand in their shoes. Poor thing, I know she hides in her religion to survive.

I didn't like anything when I first arrived in England. If you imagine you come from a village, you go to town occasionally then suddenly you're a thousand miles away from town. I had no concept of that kind of travel. I didn't want to come; I was really resentful of my mother bringing us here. It was a miserable, cold, foggy day landing at Heathrow. Because I came in the winter, every day I got up it was dark and gloomy. It was really foggy so you couldn't see for hours, couldn't see halfway down the street.

It was sort of exciting because you don't imagine it will be terribly different from where you are. You think it will be sort of the same – just wider streets, streets paved with gold. You don't understand anything about the difference of culture, how you're seen, the language, the education system and the living conditions.

I love human beings; people and their cultures fascinate me. My house was always full of people of different cultures as the kids were growing up in Willesden. It worked for us. It was fascinating for the children to be around the endless different faces, colours and hairstyles. Now, sometimes I go and stand in Leicester Square. I love it, and it's like the Tower of Babel – so many different languages.

I thought the English were cold like their weather. I thought they were bizarre-looking. When you see white people en masse, lots of pink people everywhere, strange hair and strange eyes ... it was weird.

← Yvonne Bailey-Smith with her granddaughters.

When I came here, there were the signs 'No blacks, No dogs, No Irish'. I left home when I was 17 and I would ring up in response to an advert for accommodation and put on my best English accent but when I got there the room would be gone.

YVONNE BAILEY-SMITH

```
Room to let

ring ring, ring ring
hello, my name is Bailey
I saw your add for a room
to let.

is the room still available?
yes

sorry the room is gone

yes

oh I am sorry, the room is gone

yes

I am so sorry, the room is gone

yes

Oh, I am really very sorry
the room is gone.  I am afraid
we let it to a young woman who
rang earlier.

yes
but to be honest, we don't let
rooms to blacks.
I am sorry.




            Y.A. Bailey-Smith
            1972
```

↑ An immigrant reading a racist sign on a boarding house door, 1958.

Arrival 25

SWARN KAUR BAINS
MACHINIST, HOUSEWIFE AND MOTHER OF SIX

I was 22 years old when I married my husband in a match arranged by my parents in 1951. My husband was a head teacher in Punjab. I studied to level 5 in secondary school and then took up a teaching assistant post at a military school. I taught sewing, cooking and knitting to young women. Eventually, I got married to someone from the only other educated family in our area.

Although we were successful in India, my husband eventually decided that we might be better off in England. He went first and I remember the farewell and my three small children crying as he left. For the next three years, I prayed every day and night for a letter to confirm our reunion. My mother-in-law created problems for me at times. I was beginning to feel the day would never come until in early October 1963 I was given the news that we would be leaving for England.

On 26 October 1963 we set off. I had never been outside Punjab and the journey across India took a full three days. I boarded the ship from Mumbai to Genoa with my three children. There were many Sikhs on the ship and we shared the same cabin area and were provided with Indian food at set times. People often ask me how I managed with young children and heavy pieces of luggage including a huge metal trunk. We all supported each other. Even the white passengers helped. Passing through the Suez Canal was so memorable and we saw Malta, Messina and Genoa.

On 11 November 1963 we took the ferry to Dover. I recognised my husband's voice from the barriers but I didn't expect the way he looked, dressed in a bowler hat and suit. How he looked, the weather, the people, the accommodation … everything was strange.

Everything in England was new. The roads, houses, buses, the weather, as well as 'English' clothes, language and mannerisms were all new to me. My children often

The hardest part of leaving was saying goodbye to my parents. I knew this would be our final farewell and it was. I was never to see them again. This was true for so many people who left India at the time. I was never to see my parents again and this was probably the saddest loss in my life.

ask me how I coped caring for six children (my two youngest daughters and son were born in England), and no washing machine or dishwasher, coal heating and no means of getting by other than a pram/pushchair to take the children out in. This was not an issue, hard though it was. We never had these things in India and in those days you just had to get on with life.

My eldest son wet himself when he started school because we had not taught him how to ask if he could go to the toilet in English!

Getting used to the new life was helped by the fact that my husband knew what we had to do. He worked all the hours and I looked after the house and children. However, when we bought our house I also needed to work as money was very tight. I could not work in education, which was where I worked in India. You just had to take whatever you could get.

My eldest daughter helped me a lot with household chores and managing the other children. Our relatives and lodger helped by either taking the children to school or caring for them before going to nursery. We all pulled together. It was hard but it was also one of the happiest periods of my life. My husband was working nights to make more money. During the weekends, my time was spent food shopping (we had no car), sewing and knitting clothes for the children.

← Swarn with her children Jagmohan and Rajinder.

↑ National Association of Indian Youth Building, Southall High Street, 1977.

↑ Two generations, Southall, 1977.

Although we were one of the first families in the Ilford area, over time other relatives came. Today the area is mainly Asian but in the early days if you saw an Indian you felt so pleased that you would cross the road to say hello. Over time we had many close relatives and friends living nearby. There were a number of us getting used to life here at the same time and we were able to get together and help each other.

We stayed close to our culture and religion through speaking Punjabi at home. I made sure all my children were fluent in Punjabi, we made regular visits to the Gurdwara, I prayed day and night at home, and I wore Indian clothes and ate Indian food.

I began to question my cultural beliefs and values more as my children became increasingly independent. They all got accepted by prestigious universities and this was a great source of pride, especially when it came to arranging marriages, which was my intention. However, having boyfriends before marriage; and choosing partners from different cultures was a constant source of worry and sometimes arguments. But my husband and I learnt to accept what our children wanted.

When I found work in a pickle factory, for years my daily routine was: wake up at 5.30am; prepare and take my children to school; leave the house at 7am to start work at 7.30am; leave work at 5pm and come home to feed the children; give them a bath; clean the house; and eventually go to sleep at 9.30pm. I would be very tired by the end of the day. I eventually went to work in a pyjama factory owned by a local Jewish family. They were kind to me but people could not say my name, so they called me Susan.

After my husband died, I did feel lonely and vulnerable. But one of my daughters moved into the family house. This was of some help but not the way it would have been in India, where everyone would have lived together. But I was able to accept all that came my way as I did when I first made the decision to move and settle with my children and husband in a foreign country.

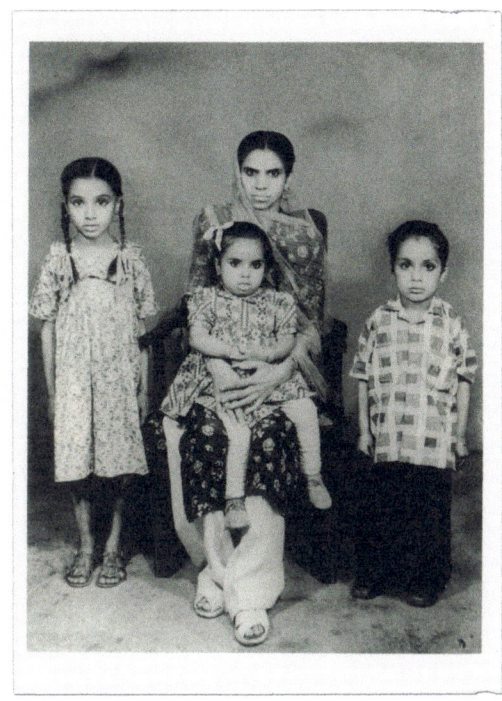

↑ Swarn Bains with her eldest children, Satinder, Rani and Gurnek.

↓ Shoppers in Southall, 1977.

When I found work in a pickle factory, for years my daily routine was: wake up at 5.30am; prepare and take my children to school; leave the house at 7am to start work at 7.30am; leave work at 5pm and come home to feed the children; give them a bath; clean the house; and eventually go to sleep at 9.30pm. I would be very tired by the end of the day. I eventually went to work in a pyjama factory owned by a local Jewish family. They were kind to me but people could not say my name, so they called me Susan.

We had to put the money in a meter for the water, lighting, gas and everything, which we were so naive about. There were no blankets, nothing. So we just slept with our overcoats on. We didn't have any money, we just had £5 and we couldn't afford to buy a blanket or anything else. All we did was buy two hot water bottles, which we could afford. So when we went to sleep or were sitting in the house, we used to just hold on to hot water bottles.

↑ An immigrant employee from Pakistan at work in a spinning mill in Bradford, West Yorkshire, c.1950.

→ It was common to send for the family once a house and job had been secured. An Asian family arrive at their new house, 'Bharj' in London, 1972.

MAHESH PATEL
TEXTILE FACTORY WORKER

In those days, rich people sent their children to England for schooling, as it was considered very good at the time. So I intended to give my family a better future by coming to England.

I landed in Heathrow in 1954. I wanted to find a good job, then call my wife and two daughters to England as well.

I had told myself that I had worked hard in India so why could I not do it here.

When I arrived here, I found the people to be good people, and helpful. I first lived in a two-bed terraced house in Coventry with nine other people. I found it really cold in the winter. The only heating at that time was a single coal fire in the living room, only lit at the weekend. I did not eat home-cooked Indian food; I used to eat beans, peas or cauliflower with bread, as I didn't know how to make chapattis.

For a bath we had to go to the public baths once a week, which we had to pay to use. The queues could take over an hour sometimes. At these times I missed home a lot and would get very unsure if I could succeed. However, the people I lived with felt the same and so we would give each other moral support.

I did not understand English so the people who arrived before me in England told me to go to where you could see chimneys and ask, 'Have you got any vacancies?' Sometimes the snow would be up to my knees when I walked up to ten miles to knock on doors and ask for work. I only realised that the doors I knocked on were houses people actually lived in when they came out. I only knew two words to listen out for: yes and no. I soon realised that it was the big chimney stacks I had to go towards to look for work!

We had to put the money in a meter for the water, lighting, gas and everything, which we were so naive about. There were no blankets, nothing. So we just slept with our overcoats on. We didn't have any money, we just had £5 and we couldn't afford to buy a blanket or anything else. All we did was buy two hot water bottles, which we could afford. So when we went to sleep or were sitting in the house, we used to just hold on to hot water bottles.

As I was in need of money my first work was as a labourer digging and lifting for six weeks. I did not know at the time that there was unemployment benefit available for people. I had good fortune when I got a testing job at Courtaulds Textiles factory. I continued to work there until I retired. I worked a night shift and overtime at Courtaulds for the first three years so that I could save to buy a two-bedroomed terraced house. In the first three years of living in England, I would often get homesick when I came across hard times. I found the strength from letters from my wife, Maniben, who gave me great support and encouragement. I think this is one of the main reasons why I did not give up and go back.

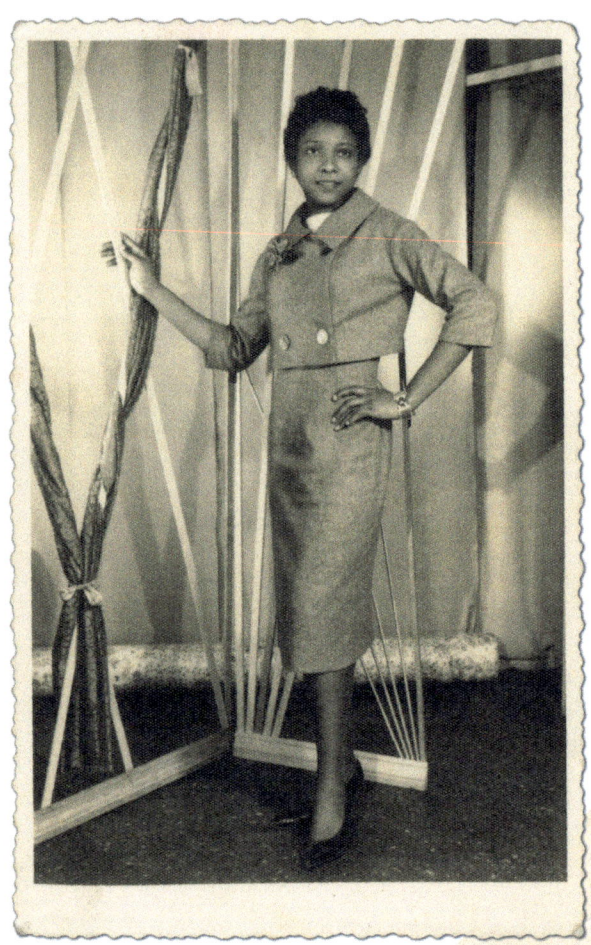

In those days we would want to be captured in our best light by the photographer at Ilona Studios and show all our folks back home how well we were doing.

MAE MILNER-BROWN
RETIRED FURTHER EDUCATION TEACHER

I came over on a boat to be looked after by a friend of my mother's, Amy Ashwood Garvey, Marcus Garvey's ex-wife. She was the owner of the house and my guardian.

I am the eldest of the three sisters and so felt responsible for my younger sisters, Lou and Val. I would keep an eye on how much sugar they were eating and make sure they kept up appearances and that sort of thing. We lived at the top of the house but would bump into the other residents on the stairs and kitchen. There were some characters in that house. There was a lesbian couple; one of them looked and dressed exactly as a man. My younger sisters did not know they were women until I told them. There was a lady from South Africa with a huge bottom who had starred in a famous movie but was clearly some sort of destitute prostitute who didn't seem to wash.

Amy, our guardian, would hold Black Power rallies in our front room but we were pretty oblivious to all the goings-on as everything was new and foreign. We took solace in laughing at people and would while away hours looking out the window or on our step checking out all the Ladbroke Grove characters passing by. We had comfort in each other and the ability to laugh.

I think the experience was really all too much for me and that is why I am affected, you know. For instance, I was without my parents and made to feel un-pretty by my carers. Granny Garvey ignored me over my housemate Cynthia because she was the light-skinned, long-legged, soft-haired one that everyone fussed over.

I think we created our own universe separate from our community. Everything was quite simple. Because we were African, we did what our parents expected of us. Our direction was to just focus on our study. We weren't challenging anything. On the other hand, the West Indians in our school were not like that at all. They had already gone into rebel mode. We were just more disciplined and perhaps more confident, I suppose. It was also a class thing. I also remember the kids at the piano group where there was a black teacher would behave better than they did with the white school where they couldn't care less. Black people don't treat the children with this liberal sort of mentality. They would not stand for misbehaviour and would just beat the hell out of them, keep them in check.

We had no real community but there were trips to the seaside on a coach organised by our music group. We would go out dressed to the hilt. The funny thing was, no one would ever set foot in the water! We would load up our coach with rice and peas and whatnot and go to the beach. Sometimes we would go to local parties and clubs where black people would congregate as a community. Pop singers used to go there like Dusty Springfield and her black girlfriend. But the worst ones were the church dos. We were dragged there by Granny Garvey and we would just sit there.

Later I moved to Cambridge. The teachers at college made me feel welcome. The older brother of the man who wrote *A Man for All Seasons* fancied me. Subsequently I met him on a plane on the way to Ghana, many years later. He was going to visit his Ghanaian wife, so I guess I inspired him.

← Mae Milner-Brown taken at Studio Photo Ilona.

← The sisters Valerie, Lou and Mae.

I had seen the white people, the British people, in my country as rulers. They used to have a lot of servants – nannies, gardeners, cooks and butlers. When I came to Heathrow Airport, I saw a couple of white guys mopping the floor and I was really shocked because I thought: you know, the black people, like the servant people who were ruled over by the British, would be doing those jobs. Driving to Bradford I also saw many white people doing minor jobs, like roadworks. I couldn't believe what I was seeing!

SULTAN MAHMOOD, FIRST MAGISTRATE OF PAKISTANI ORIGIN IN BRITAIN

← Mr T Sullivan, a road sweeper in Markyate, Hertfordshire, 1957.

→ Francis Quadras holds up his British passport on arrival at Luton Airport from Kenya, 1968. He is one of hundreds of Kenyan Asians who arrived in Britain just before the passing of the British Government's Emergency Bill, which aimed to limit the number of migrants coming into the country.

Asian workers, on whom many of the present foundries depend seen working their last shift at Bullers Foundry, Sandwell, West Midlands, 1983.

CHAPTER TWO

HARD LABOUR

Caribbeans were told to come to the motherland to get an education and make a better life. They were not psychologically prepared for what they would meet. They were beaten down, ground down. They couldn't use their skills. My mother was a fantastic designer. She was not prepared for the life here, and it was hard.

YVONNE BAILEY-SMITH

Leicester, 1974. One of many Asians who came to work in the factories in the Midlands.

CHAPTER TWO

HARD LABOUR

THE SURVIVAL GRIND

The immigrant search for a better life often involves sacrifice at an emotional, practical and logistical level.

In this chapter, we explore the sacrifice that many Indians and Afro-Caribbeans endured by having to work in tedious, menial, low-paid jobs in order to carve out a new life in a new country. Many of those jobs, like sweeping chimneys and work in sweatshops, have largely been eradicated today thanks to significant progress in human rights and industry regulation. However, desperation has, and no doubt always will, made immigrants an easy target for exploitation.

Deception often started before immigrants set foot on British soil. To obtain the necessary passports or visas, people were required to signify professions or trade qualifications that were desirable in Britain. The deception here was twofold. Immigrants were motivated to say they had whatever qualification allowed them entry, and officials signing off passports and visas were known to encourage this deception or at least turn a blind eye to it. That said, overqualification was just as much if not more of an issue than underqualification. Doctors, lawyers and teachers often found that their credentials, no matter how prestigious in their own country, were not recognised in Britain because they were gained in non-British institutions. Consequently, immigrants often found it impossible to get work in their professional area once they arrived in Britain. At the same time, people with no formal skills or qualifications were being signed off as mechanics or engineers, for example. Menial, hard-labour jobs, particularly those which involved punishing night shifts, were the easiest, and often the only, work for newcomers to find.

More often than not, immigrants took this in their stride. It was not uncommon for people to be working back-to-back night and day shifts in several jobs. Again and again, we heard stories of hardship and resilience that came as a surprise, even to the sons and daughters of the immigrants themselves. Rather than whingeing, self-pity or resentment, there was an acceptance and understanding by these early pioneers that hard labour was a necessary and valuable sacrifice for their families in order to give them a better chance at what life could offer. In many senses, this constituted a long-term plan of self-sacrifice, particularly with respect to the Asian immigrants. In general, we found that Asians seemed to have a clearer vision of what they wanted to achieve over time than the Afro-Caribbeans. This may have been because they had more of a community around them and various role models of hard work.

Unions were established for the underprivileged theoretically to help ensure fair pay and conditions for workers. However, the unions were often racially prejudiced and therefore ambivalent about how black people were treated. Consequently, some black people formed alternative unions that would more genuinely fight for their rights. In any case, pay and conditions were almost universally poor so the more entrepreneurial immigrants would set up their own businesses, typically corner shops and small restaurants.

Today, the impact of the migrant hard-work ethic is evident in many areas of life across the UK. The NHS employs huge numbers of ethnic minority staff, who support the purpose of this critical institution. Corner shops and restaurants still abound, providing convenience and delicious food to local communities. Some start-ups have become large, thriving businesses, such as Bestway and Patak's, employing thousands of people in the UK and abroad. Shifts in education league tables have also reflected the migrant work ethic with Indian and Afro-Caribbean children now outperforming working-class white populations across the country.

I remember a lot of people who had law degrees and master's education from India and Pakistan; they were working as a bus conductor. SULTAN MAHMOOD

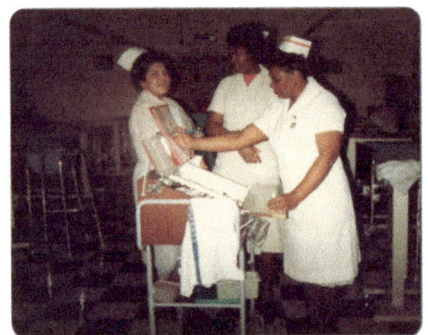

↑ Two workers of Pakistani origin in a cloth mill near Bradford, 1989. Most Pakistani migrants came to Britain in the 1950s and 60s when their manpower was needed for the booming cloth industry.

← Dorothy Young, now a retired nurse as a young mother and with her colleagues in the NHS. She came to London from Jamaica in 1960.

→ At Peckham Bus Garage, South London, September 1958. West Indian bus drivers were the liveliest act in town! A working-class job made fabulous with their typically vibrant and easy-going ways.

Asians expelled from Uganda often arrived penniless after being robbed by General Amin's soldiers and officials. Here a couple arrives at their new home in London, 1972.

The strange thing is that because you didn't know about racism you didn't realise what was happening.

DELORIS SMITH

Let's talk about Covid-19. It's interesting that the people on the front line – that's the bus drivers, nurses – got ill with all the systemic racism going on. We are told they are heroes but I don't think they were saying, 'Don't worry, I'll work extra', it was the people that had to, didn't have any other choice. My friend whom I know from school said how scared they were driving these buses, but they couldn't not go to work: it was their work ethic as well as their need for a livelihood.

JENNI FRANCIS, ART EXPERT AND INTERNATIONAL MUSEUM PROFESSIONAL

My mum worked for the NHS and her working nights was all I knew. She would plait our hair before going off to work so we were ready in the morning.

JENNI FRANCIS

As a nursing student you would come in and you were supposed to get a daily report. But if the matron was racist and you hadn't been given the report, she would tell you to go and get it yourself. The sisters on the ward would exclude you from the group case studies. They would create an exclusive club, in a sneaky way. I would go in there and have a read of the reports myself. You couldn't be confrontational.

DELORIS SMITH

Asians expelled from Uganda arrive at London's Heathrow Airport, 1972.

ERROL TURNER
SHIPPING AGENT AND AVID DOMINOES PLAYER

I have worked as a shipping agent since about 1988. Before that I went from building site to building site, doing labouring work. After that I got into more managerial work, with Taylor Woodrow to be exact. I was travelling, going about all the building and measuring up the amount of bricks used. If it were a nine-inch wall, it would be double bricks – all that had to be logged along with the name of the site, etc. I would go all over the country, night and day on the road till it got too much for me. I went all over the continent. Went to Saudi Arabia. I wanted to see what it was like, but nobody wanted the post. Now I see why. The sandstorm would be racking up on the cabin. I had to lock myself in the cabin.

I packed up that job and went into the Post Office as a postman. In those days you had to go to Post Office school for just two weeks. If you pass, you can go to the sorting office; if you fail, you are out. I saved enough to buy a property in Wembley for my girlfriend who was expecting a baby. I bought another property in Harrow Road but sold them both. I had enough to give my daughter some money and managed to go back to Jamaica, as my parents were sick.

I personally have never encountered any problems with the English. As I said, I used to work on building sites. A friend of mine one day said, 'I have this eight-foot crate.' It was very heavy. It was made out of three-quarter-inch ply. He said, 'How am I going to get it in the van?' I said, 'Watch me.' I picked up the crate and stood it on its end upright on cardboard so it doesn't damage, I reversed the van up to the crate then tipped the top of the crate into the van and then pushed my back up against it, pushed it into the van.

As a matter of fact, when I got my job at Taylor Woodrow, I remember at my first job interview there were three of us waiting for an interview and I was the only black man and I got the job. I didn't even have a tie on like the others. The man said to me, 'Mr Turner as long as you are clean and tidy – I just want somebody who knows what they are doing.' He said to me, 'I apologise to keep you waiting. You went to school in Jamaica, didn't you? You can do algebra.' Maths was my best subject at school. 'Those men in front of you went to school here and they can't do algebra. I asked them what is 100 minus 4 and they started using their fingers!'

So, the shipper, an Englishman, Paul, said, 'Mr Turner, why don't you do the shipping yourself?' I said, 'I don't know where to start.' He took out some letter-headed paper and said, 'Look, get a few cards and paper like that with your name and address or whatever you want to call yourself.' And that is what I have done.

My motto is: work hard, relax and enjoy yourself. Life is funny: one minute you are up and one minute you are down. Be strong and you will get back up there again. I see people walking around looking half dead but you gotta work hard, being negative doesn't work. Not with me anyway. Be positive in anything you are doing. I say I am going to do this and I am going to get there.

← Errol runs a Friday night dominoes club. He is seen here wearing the baseball cap.

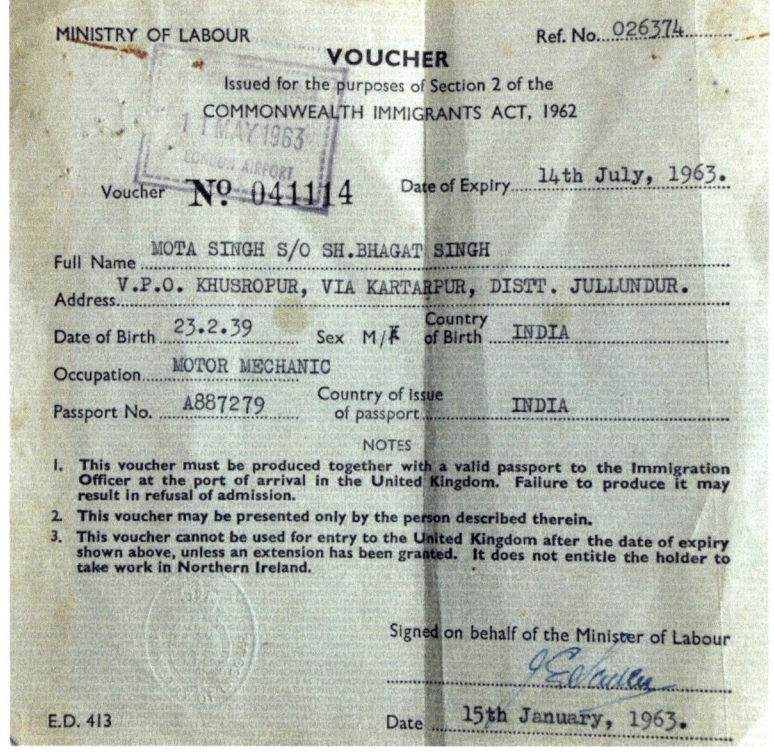

→ Mota Singh's passport photos.

← The required immigration voucher for settlement in the UK, 1962.

MOTA SINGH
FOUNDRY AND
POST OFFICE
WORKER, POET
AND POLITICIAN

I did work in the foundry but I tell you they were the worst days of my life. We were given a job on the grinding machines and it was not a small thing; it took two people to lift it. It was very hard work. I didn't remove my turban. It was nothing to do with religion but I was very determined not to.

May 1963. There were no jobs. My problem was also that I didn't want to ruin my turban and 90 per cent of Punjabis had to take their turbans off at work.

I knew my cousin was here and a few relatives, so I stayed in Slough for three weeks. Because of the goodness of these people, any person coming from Punjab could stay in any house and they would never charge you anything for food, drinks or accommodation. They also helped you if you needed to send some money back home.

I looked for work in Slough for about a year, but then I moved to Leamington. After three months there, someone helped get me a job in a polishing company. I was given the dirtiest job. They made small parts for motors and you had to put a mask on your face, but there was no proper health and safety.

That job didn't last long because one day the boss came in and stopped the machine and said, 'Those who want to join the union – out. If you are not joining the union then you can stay.' So five of us went to Coventry to the union office and they told us not to worry and asked us if we wanted to work in the foundry.

I did work in the foundry but I tell you they were the worst days of my life. We were given a job on the grinding machines and it was not a small thing; it took two people to lift it. It was very hard work. I didn't remove my turban. It was nothing to do with religion but I was very determined not to.

Most places would ask you to take your turban off, but that foundry job didn't. But it was very hard work. Not long hours as the motor industry was wealthy, but very hard work. The feeling was that it was good money. I remember that if you worked nights you got £25, and the other factory work was £11–12. Then I became seriously ill because of chest problems from working in the foundry. I worked there for four years before going to India to get married. When I came back, I couldn't find a job again. Three times I tried to get a job in the Post Office. They said, 'No, Mr Singh, you don't fit with our uniform, you have to take your turban off.' Getting a job on the railways, in a post office, on the buses – there were no turbans allowed. They finally accepted me in the Post Office in 1974. I was very pleased and I enjoyed it, but the wages were 50 per cent lower than at Ford.

I worked as a postman for 28 years until I retired. My hard experience of work made me interested in improving the conditions of Asian workers. I started doing community work, after working a long day at the Post Office. I worked actively for the Sikh community and got involved with associations helping to advance the conditions of Asian and black workers.

I also became interested in political work and in 1985 I was elected to the Warwickshire County Council for the Labour Party. I was on my own there for 16 years and there was no second Asian. It is very sad that after 24 years there is not a single black person on the Council. I can't complain though about my own treatment. I became a member of the Police Authority and eventually Chairman. Then, in 2004, I was elected to be Mayor of Leamington. It was a great breakthrough for the Asian community there.

My life has been tough but I have kept myself going. I have used my hardships to inspire myself and others to do more. It is sad that young Asians these days do not seem so interested in public service at the local level.

I have had great sadness in my life as well. My wife passed away before she could see me become Mayor. Then in 2007, my beloved son Gurpreet (Gilly) died. He was only 36 and it was a total shock for all of us. But I resolved to do something to preserve his memory. We worked hard to raise money and found the Gilly Mundy Community School, in his honour, in Haryana, India.

↑ Immigrant workers at Repton Foundry Ltd near Bradford.

→ Blast furnaces at a steel mill at Halifax in Yorkshire.

Southall sorting office, 1974.

Near Bradford. In a cloth mill, a Pakistani stops work for his evening prayer, a practice condoned by few firms in Britain.

SWARN KIRPAL
RADIO NEWS PRESENTER, SCHOOLTEACHER AND SUB-POST OFFICE MANAGER

I was 12 years old and living in Lahore when we went through Partition, which was very sad, very sudden and very difficult. The girl siblings were threatened with rape, so we fled from Lahore in the middle of the night with a sewing machine.

My family were freedom fighters and used to visit the prison and go on rallies and my uncle was given a plaque from Gandhi which we still have.

My husband and I were lucky to have a 'love marriage' and had a happy life in India. He came to England before me to get any job he could find. He had to lie and say he had experience in order to get a job in the Ford motor factory, but they made him do night shifts.

I had done a teaching course in India but then I won a competition on the All India Radio station, so I became a radio presenter. I loved it as they used to pick me up from my house in a big car which was very glamorous. But then my father told me I should resign and go to England to be with my husband. In those days people would travel by ship but my husband sent for me and my baby son by air. We were looked after very well on the flight, not like today where everyone pushes past you and you feel like you are being squashed onto a Tube train.

When I arrived in England, I felt more inclined to work in radio rather than teaching, so I went to the BBC and had an audition to become a broadcaster. They said my English was perfect but they had no vacancies. So I applied to become a teacher and was told they would call me when there was a vacancy. By the time I did hear back I had already had another child. My daughter was only three months old then but they really wanted me to start teaching at a nearby nursery.

I taught at a school in Hackney for ten years and I would wear my sari to work, but in the winter it would get wet in the snow. I asked if I could wear trousers, but they said no and that I could only wear English skirts or my traditional Indian dress. I wouldn't wear skirts, so I had to keep getting my sari wet.

Being a teacher was sometimes very hard as the children would make fun of me and say, 'Oh, she can actually write' when I was writing on the board. It is so different to India. There the students are so respectful and see the teachers as gurus.

I learnt so much about English culture from my work as a teacher through the children's stories that we used at the school. It was very helpful. In our country, you didn't even look directly at your elders, not even your parents, because this was a sign of respect. But here, it is very different.

One day, I was at the school and a teacher was trying to help one of the students. He kept looking at the floor and the teacher said to him, 'Look me in the eye when I am talking to you!' I just thought, 'Oh my God, what is that?'

My daughter was being looked after well at the nursery but one day they came to me and said they were having problems with her.

They said she had been asking for something called 'paki'. They gave her milk and juice, but she actually just wanted water. I told the staff that 'pani' means water in Punjabi and so they told me that she needed elocution

Being a teacher was sometimes very hard as the children would make fun of me and say, 'Oh, she can actually write' when I was writing on the board. It is so different to India. There the students are so respectful and see the teachers as gurus.

The Kirpals' house in Leyton.

lessons and she should speak the Queen's English. They also told me not to speak my language in front of my daughter and I must only speak English to her. Nowadays my daughter asks why we didn't teach her Punjabi.

We settled in well in England, but people asked if they could call my husband and I 'Sonia and Ron' because it was easier than our real names, Swarn and Ranvir.

In the early years, we didn't really get to know our neighbours, but we would meet nice people in the street. Some would give a few shillings to my baby in the pram because they said it was good luck. I never felt racism or people talking down to me. I always felt it was fair.

Everything was a struggle, we were poor, and we had mice in the house. Then one day we won the Football Pools, which is like the Lottery. Three men came to the door to tell my husband and even though he could have taken all the money, he shared it with the two other men who split the bets with him. With the winnings we decided to set up a sub-post office on Lea Bridge Road in Leyton.

That went well most of the time, but we did get robbed a few times. The first time a black man shot at me in the shop but I ducked and he hit the wall behind me making a hole in the wall. The Post Office gave me an honours and bravery award.

The second time involved the whole family. Two white men beat my husband up, they hit him with a gun and tried to force him to open the safe, but he told them it was on a timer so they gave up. They tied up my son and threw my daughter down the stairs. She was only nine years old and wet herself.

Also, they asked me to lie on the floor face down. Thankfully our neighbours, who were wondering why white men were in our flat, had called the police and the robbers ending up running off.

We've seen so much really. You do things in life with a straight mind. You can't think of crime and criminals all the time. Otherwise, what is life?

My nephew, Sharat, was a writer for the TV show *Goodness Gracious Me* and he based some of the characters on people in our family. I was Mrs Eat More!

↑↓ At the Golden Temple, Amritsar, 1957.

The Shafi in Gerrard Street was one of the first Indian restaurants in Britain. It opened in 1920.

They used to call us names saying, 'Oh, you stink of curry.' Now they all eat it. It's the national craving now, adopted as a national dish!

SHAZARDI HASHMI
RETIRED FACTORY WORKER

My husband would often find they would write, 'Paki go home' on his clocking-in card. He never got promoted and white guys did. He didn't say anything about this to us for a long time because he didn't want to upset us.

My husband had a terrible time at work. He worked as a maintenance engineer with a switchgear company called Rosen & Co. He was the only skilled worker of Pakistani origin and this created a lot of hostility among the English workers. He didn't talk about it at the time but he would be abused and was attacked, and called names on a daily basis.

I stayed at home looking after the children. It was difficult to know what was going on as most of the other Pakistanis in the neighbourhood were single men and I was cut off. I felt sad and lonely. Once in a while we would go to the cinema in Bradford to see an Indian film.

Things got so bad that my husband decided to send us back to Pakistan, so we went back to Lahore and lived with my mum. Life was a lot better because my family and friends were around. However, the kids kept getting ill and we decided that as bad as things had been in England, for health and the children's education, we would be better coming back.

We came back and got a house in Leeds. In those days in Leeds there were a lot of poor working-class white people and we got a lot of trouble because we were a bit richer. Every time you put clothes on the washing line, the kids would steal them. Our shed got kicked in so many times we would stop repairing it. It was worse for my two sons who were attacked all the time. One day, five white boys from the estate jumped on my son and broke his jaw with a brick.

I got a job as a machinist making toiletries at Elida Gibbs. It was a tough life getting up at 4am every day, getting to work at 6am and leaving at 2pm to cook, clean and look after the family. The work was tough and I developed a really bad back, so much so I had to give up work.

We decided to go into business and started making ready-made frozen Indian food to sell to shops and for events. My son, who was only 15 was running it, but he got taken in by some older Pakistani workers. These guys would take the food and sell it themselves without telling us. We lost a lot of money and decided to close the business.

Although things were bad for a long time, our lives gradually improved. People got used to having Pakistanis around and older people used to be against us but now are friends. All my children are settled and have good jobs. Things are so different now. My granddaughter now just feels English and has never suffered the kind of things we went through.

I got a job as a machinist making toiletries at Elida Gibbs. It was a tough life getting up at 4am every day, getting to work at 6am and leaving at 2pm to cook, clean and look after the family. The work was tough and I developed a really bad back, so much so I had to give up work.

CHAPTER THREE

CONNECTING WITH THE LOCALS

I am a stranger to no one;
and no one is a stranger to me.
Indeed, I am a friend to all.
GURU GRANTH SAHIB, P. 1299

CHAPTER THREE

CONNECTING WITH THE LOCALS

GETTING TO KNOW YOU

Today, Britain is self-evidently mixed-race, international and cosmopolitan, and tourists flock to revel in this diversity.

Britain has allowed immigrants to make contributions, and recognises and celebrates achievers. British sporting heroes and heroines, from the Olympics to Wimbledon and of course on the football field, hail from all parts of the globe. Likewise, Britain is proud of home-grown foodie talents like Jamie Oliver, Gordon Ramsay and Nigel Slater, as well as culinary stars like Madhur Jaffrey, Ainsley Harriott and Anjum Anand.

Essentially, and perhaps predictably, there was a huge variation in the experience of early immigrants and in the way the British reacted to them. Some British people were hostile toward outsiders, but we also heard stories of warmth, generosity and welcome, of the British genuinely going out of their way to support and learn about newcomers to their shores.

On the whole, it's apparent that there is a very special attitude among the British compared to other host communities. Britain is an island, and perhaps because of this it is particularly good at absorbing and integrating others. It is hard to imagine, for example, the French embracing curry as their national dish!

Britain's relationship with its migrants was often a multifaceted phenomenon whereby you could have a BNP (British National Party) or EDL (English Defence League) member with a Sikh or black person as his or her best friend! Arguably, the residual effects of Britain's colonial background led to the schizophrenic nature of things as they now are.

It has been a struggle for the Commonwealth migrants who came here not knowing how unwanted they would be. Disrupting the British idea of themselves and their country has had ramifications. With regularity the National Front skinheads would make attacks on migrants, including the horrific murder of teenager Gurdip Singh Chaggar in 1976.

Without a good grasp of postcolonial history it is easy to believe that most migrants are being given handouts or a leg-up.

The response to this racism eventually came with the Indian Workers' Association running campaigns for workers' rights and other equality issues.

Southall and the Borough of Ealing were trailblazers in changing culture in the 1960s; there were protests and struggles to assert some basic care for immigrants' welfare and well-being which has paved the way for a thriving community of Indian businesses and has contributed to the cultural life there.

An international human rights campaign, which highlighted a number of international crises, aimed at eliminating racial discrimination in the UK, and to help people from dependent territories to realise their human rights. Councillor and Mayor of Ealing Percy Southey raised support in 1968 for a programme of activities and projects among local education bodies, churches, societies, students, trade unions, the Rotary Club, women's organisations and youth clubs to promote racial cohesion.

Without a good grasp of postcolonial history it is easy to believe that most migrants are being given handouts or a leg-up.

← Watching Notting Hill Carnival, London, 1975.

Immigrants were perfect scapegoats for lack of housing, NHS queues, degradation of the streets and crime. However, the predominantly white areas of Southall and Ealing in the 1960s were terrorised by white teenagers before the newcomers arrived. They were causing as much civil disobedience as young black youths are accused of today. Knife crime before the 1980s was infighting between skinheads and Rockabillies in ritual gang warfare. However, the same agitated youth paved the way for the multicultural Britain we have today.

One correspondent in the *Southall and County Times* pointed out that the teenagers in the youth clubs are 'setting a good example to the older generation by making friends with all the coloured people of the borough'.

↑ Church leaders and MPs in a March for Unity in Southall, 1976.

→ Southall Carnival 1977: the ethos reflected the concerns of the white community. The pre-existing community had strong feelings against migration.

Organisations such as the Coloured People's Progressive Association and the Racial Adjustment Action Society were founded in the wake of the riots and broke new ground for black Britons.

→ Southall residents riot after the murder of Gurdip Singh Chaggar. Many refer to it as 'the first uprising'.

↓ Protesting against the racist rhetoric of Enoch Powell, which inflamed hatred for migrants among the British.

Britain's relationship with its migrants was often a multifaceted phenomenon whereby you could have a BNP or EDL member with a Sikh or black person as his or her best friend! Arguably, the residual effects of Britain's colonial background led to the schizophrenic nature of things as they now are.

The impact of the Brixton riots should not be understated. The idea that black people could stage an insurrection in the heart of the capital was significant. It was definitely seen as a political gesture and made British politicians take racism and racial injustice seriously for the first time. The riots created a climate in which it was possible for myself and three others to be the first black people elected to Parliament in 1987. All of the advances that black people have made in the past 25 years owe something to the fact that young black people took to the streets.

DIANE ABBOTT MP

↑ Southall Broadway Sikhs protest against troubles in Punjab, 1978.

↑ Smithfield meat porters march on the Home Office, with a petition calling for an end to all immigration into Britain, August 1972.

Local residents walk past a burnt-out pub in Brixton after a second night of rioting in the area, April 1981.

The people who lived here were pretty much ghettoised at the time but went on to shape a way of life that encompassed a party spirit as well as a community activism that paved the way for immigrant voices to be listened to.

RETIRED SCHOOLTEACHER JOSETTE LYNCH
TALKING ABOUT MOSS SIDE, MANCHESTER

← Wolverhampton children playing, 1978.

↓ A Notting Hill Carnival float raises a tribute to the *Empire Windrush* – the first boat of immigrants from the West Indies in 1948.

Before the film stars and celebrities moved into this exotic playground, Ladbroke Grove and Notting Hill were home to a vibrant colony of bohemians, bookies, drug dealers and misfits.

Notting Hill, known as Notting Dale then, was the insalubrious dwelling of the white working class before the new Caribbean settlers moved in. Notting Dale was an enclave of the most rumbustious lot, a place beyond the law. It was so run down the residents would get their weekly wash at Silchester Baths and rob their own gas meters! Illegal gambling and drinking dens, known as 'spiel and afters', appeared faster than the law could close them down. Whole families would sometimes be living in one or two rooms in these crumbling tenements with outside toilets and no bathrooms. By the 1950s, West Indian men came to Brtain in droves to 'check out the terrain'. Sometimes they would have a relative to move in with but all hoped to find homes and work so they could then send for their wives and children. Often they report of the filthy and unwelcoming city. Initially many of these men would end up finding housing in hostels like Colonial House in Kensington where many Caribbean men shared a room until they had worked long enough to rent or buy.

Locals like Lucky Gordon, Darance Licorish and Gus 'Osmond' Philip, who are interviewed here, have seen the changes over their lifetime. They describe the old area as a 'backwater full of outlaws' before the gentrification took place. There was no second body to monitor the police whose discriminatory practices were very much part of this unlawful atmosphere. Indeed, forged from the intensity of the race riots instigated by Oswald Mosley in 1958, the residents eventually found a way to live together and love aspects of each other. The trials they have gone through have honed some local characters and unsung heroes, such as the white British women who were in relationships, with black men and fought by their side in the riots of 1958 and after.

Rogue landlords, police prejudice and the difficulty of finding good jobs created a pressure cooker that exploded in an already struggling community. The Notting Hill riots of 1958 were the first of the racially charged riots that occurred all over the country, and were a watershed moment which led to the militant self-organisation of the residents. In 1981 there were riots
in Brixton, Toxteth, Handsworth and Moss Side, among other places, with the Broadwater Farm riots taking place in 1985. The Brixton riots led to the Scarman Report into what was wrong endemically. The predominantly Asian areas of Bradford and Oldham took longer to percolate, bursting into riot and protest in 2001.

The North Kensington Amenity Trust threw out a car park proposal at its first meeting with the authorities and convinced contractors working on the motorway to instead construct an adventure playground for the community in the summer of 1968. The council saw that such an organisation could access resources that it could not, particularly in terms of funding. This seemed both the best way to move from the entrenched positions of the past and the only way to get things done. That experiment would be seen as a model for a new type of local delivery body responsive to community needs and free to do things differently.

With the strong community voice Ladbroke Grove has developed through its hardship, many initiatives have helped the community to thrive. Youth culture of the 1980s, for instance, was backed by the whole community in the area, producing a major skatepark, youth clubs, street art, and perhaps the best example of powerful ground-up community action. The now world-famous Notting Hill Carnival is a British institution: tourists flock to soak up the atmosphere as it is the biggest melting pot of cultures anywhere in the world. Britain's wealthy have their city homes here; they have literally 'bought' into an area defined by the colourful migrant characters. Here in particular, the Caribbean and Indian migrants have always been clear they have brought colour and joy to a severe landscape emerging from a post-Victorian world.

Tourists flock to soak up the atmosphere of the Notting Hill Carnival as it is the biggest melting pot of cultures anywhere in the world.

*The time to be happy is now,
The place to be happy is here,
The way to be happy is to make others happy,
And to build a little heaven down here.*

SONG TAKEN FROM THE SABBATH SCHOOL, SEVENTH-DAY ADVENTIST CHURCH.

I do not bear hatred because as a Christian it is not something I can afford to do. So I find if you remain calm and friendly people will eventually come round. I worked with a teacher once who was Irish and said she had encountered a lot of racism. She said to me, 'Joss, I can't understand how you can ever love white people after all the slavery and what went on with your people thereafter.' I said, 'Yes, I know about the history and it was horrible but then you know the people alive today didn't do it so it wouldn't make sense for me to go on hating and avenge what has happened to my poor parents.'

And I do hold people up if they say wrong things and often it was out of ignorance and they admit they didn't understand why they had prejudice, they're just brainwashed, see. I listen to people like the son of Martin Luther King. When asked if he hated the people who killed his dad he said,' 'No, we have to learn to live together or we perish like fools.'

JOSETTE LYNCH

We take pride in our homes. We take pride in our dress – everyone doing it now. At church the standard is kept high. You should not be wearing trousers to church. The English dress better now for church too – they 'step up'. DOROTHY YOUNG

↓ Choir in a Pentecostal church in Brixton, London, 1975.

OVERLEAF Annual National Convention of the Black-Led Churches in England at Bingley Hall, Brimingham, where Symphony Hall now stands, 1983.

Connecting with the Locals   69

LUCKY GORDON
ALOYSIUS 'LUCKY' GORDON (1931–2017)
VALET AT ISLAND RECORDS

Notorious Lucky made tabloid headlines in 1968. In the film *Scandal*, he was portrayed as the rogue who introduced the innocent country girl Christine Keeler to an edgy party scene of sex and drugs.

After prison and before I signed up for the army, I was fighting other villains night and day. If I did not fight them, I would possibly be dead by now. I had to go all out and fight. These people were working for the Krays. The only thing for them was force. Reggie had to ask, 'What's the matter with you, you don't have respect for anyone?' But I said, 'Your men are messing around with me. In prison I got labelled as a grass.' The label of me as a grass was all over England. You can't walk the streets without something bad happening. So I had to get rid of the stigma.

The Krays sent for me, invited me to Mile End and introduced me to a lot of people. They asked me if I wanted to work in their club, the Brown Derby in Beak Street.

They wanted me to come in with them but I said no. Then they took me to this guy who collected money from loads of clubs for them. They paid him £500 every week. So, this was the start of the music business for me. I said to him, 'Why don't you turn the place into a shebeen, where you can drink, listen to some music? I know a man in Ladbroke Grove called Count Suckle who can bring down a huge following.' Count Suckle started doing a show; it became so popular. He had Errol Watson as a resident band and later Georgie Fame and I sang with him. I introduced Duke Vin to them too.

There are stories from my time that have never been told. Kelso Cochrane was killed by the police. Nobody knows what I know. No Teddy Boys did it, that was a cover-up by the police. Things were a lot harder before the 1958 riots.

The police would have names on lists and wait for the opportunity to throw them in the Thames. They'd say the gangsters were doing it, but there were no gangsters doing it. They'd say Teddy Boys started the riots. It was the police all the way. It was terrible what the police were doing – dirty work.

I left London two days before the Notting Hill riots of 1958. The police wanted me out the way. One day before the riot the police got an informer to accuse me of larceny. They beat me so bad they almost killed me and when I was in hospital that's when the riot started. I was in hospital for almost 13 days. I had a thousand petrol bottles with a wick in them, lined up on top of Blenheim Crescent because I knew something serious was going to happen. The police started it and not only that, they were murdering quite a few of us!

I used to tell the average black man who was hustling on the road, 'When the police pull you up at night, make a whole load of noise so that people know you are out there and realise you are going to jail so they can inquire about you at night. Otherwise they knock you out and throw you in the Thames and say that villains did it. They already did that with a couple of my friends.'

What we used to do, we used to go out and beat the police. I'm not joking, we used to go out at night and get the better of them 'cause they were attacking us in the day. There was a policeman who used to put all of us in jail. Not me, 'cause he was terrified of me. He wants my friend to turn informer and he said no. That friend went missing and I got nervous so I began to look for him … would go up and down, went looking for him night and day and I had a sawn-off with me and I would use it on him (the policeman). The owner of the Mangrove took it off me in the end.

← The infamous Profumo affair: Lucky Gordon outside court.

I met Christine Keeler in a café they call the Rio, just down the road. We went to the Mangrove, a restaurant and hangout in All Saints Road, and as soon as I pass the door I get this magical feeling about me and then I get glued to the spot. As I turn my head to the right I see her with two gentlemen. My friend says to me, 'Have you never seen a woman before?'

Stephen Ward was one of the men she was with. I watched them and saw he got Christine to settle a 'draw' [marijuana] for them. She got up and went downstairs to go and get the smoke. She was standing by the toilet and I followed her. I said to her, 'I know all the guys around here and I will get the best for you.' When I came back to her with the stuff, I said, 'I don't understand how a beautiful girl like you can smoke.' She said she liked to every now and then, and when can she see me to get more. Keeler said, 'I tell you what is even more interesting – if you try to get a black girl for my brother and we will make it a foursome.' I am a rude boy, don't forget, so I set about it. There are not many black women in those days but I had a friend called Kit who had a beautiful wife. I go to his house and told him the situation and said I need to introduce her and that nothing will come of her, and she will be back home soon. He let that happen 'cause he was frightened of me.

So the next day I call Christine and we arranged to meet at the Odeon Westbourne Grove. They turn up in this white Jaguar. Christine and Stephen Ward. That's whom she was talking about; her brother was supposedly Stephen Ward. So I get in the back with Christine and the girl in the front with Stephen Ward. Straight away he started touching the girl I had brought and straight away she said, 'I'm getting out.' He instantly made an excuse, said he had to get back so nothing came of that night.

The next night Christine wanted to come to a blues dance with me. Stephen Ward would try to hang out and get me to get a smoke but I didn't like him hanging around. We see each other regularly. She was no prostitute; she was a good-time girl. They did that so they could get the conviction under way.

↑ Lucky Gordon in the 1980s.

I am not ashamed to tell you I used to service a lot of men's wives. We were all entertaining wives.

→ Lucky's photo album snaps, of him in Jamaica and one on Hampstead Heath, London.

There is an album called *The Affair* released by Island Records. One day I went to a junk shop and found my voice on this satirical record. You can imagine my surprise when I hear my voice impersonated on the record, which was a huge success. I asked the owner of the record label, Chris Blackwell, for money but he said there was not enough royalty to give me as a recording artist. I started to terrorise him now, saying he couldn't go back to Jamaica. Chris offered me a job at Island Records. The whole Keeler scandal was out and against me so in actual fact I found sanctuary in the place. I had connections in Jamaica for Chris.

I cooked for the groups and Chris Blackwell … everything to do with taking care of the artists like Bob Marley, etc., rolled into one. I get to record, sing jazz in the studio now.

A heady mix of upper-class revellers quite literally rubbing shoulders with the new and vibey Caribbeans who were the lifeblood of these parties providing marijuana and girls. Lucky feels that his notorious media image – that of a pimp – twisted his relationship with Keeler. For him, it was a tender love story.

← Lucky outside the Old Bailey, 1963.

↑ The infamous Mangrove restaurant, where Christine Keeler met Lucky Gordon. Many other seminal moments in cultural life happened here which put the All Saints Road on the map. Socialites and celebrities came to the venue to party with the West Indian party scene and of course the marijuana suppliers.

Connecting with the Locals

A Bangladeshi family in the kitchen of their rented semi-detached home in Smethwick, West Midlands, 1983. The second wave of immigrants, they suffered the worst housing conditions.

KAMALA SHARMA
MACHINIST

Our experience of English people was mostly positive. They were very nice people in Hull, very nice people.

Even the neighbours came to greet us and to say that we were welcome to the neighbourhood. They said, 'Anything you want, come and ask for it.'

Then it was Christmas time and everybody posted Christmas cards through the letterbox. One of the English neighbours actually came and invited us for a Christmas lunch. They came and picked us up from our house and they also dropped us home in the evening. We were very welcome.

We were the first Ugandan Asians to settle in Hull. After us, about three families came, that's all. We were quite a minority. My husband became very popular in his job. I also became popular and started to progress.

Unfortunately, I fell ill with a burst appendix and there was a strike at the time, so there were no ambulances. We didn't have a telephone in the house, so my husband had to go out and make a phone call to a doctor. He came and he said we have to rush her to hospital otherwise she is going to die in half an hour. It was very critical. We didn't have anyone to take us to the hospital and my husband just went to the next-door neighbour and asked if he could order a taxi, which was very difficult for us to afford. The neighbour told him not to worry; he would take us to the hospital. When I was discharged, he came and picked me up after a week. I didn't know that I had to send a sick note or things like that, so my job was lost after three weeks when I recovered. I went back and they said, 'You've lost your job because you didn't inform us.' I told them I didn't know but they said they needed a sick note.

We never looked back. Now we've got our own house, other properties and our own car, we are quite comfortable. We go on holiday every year.

When we came to London, obviously it's a big city so people were in their own worlds and we rented a garage room, where my son was born. We paid £16 a week just for that garage where we had to sleep, eat, drink, cook, sit, watch TV, whatever.

That was the only room we had and we had to share the bathroom and the toilet with the landlord. We had to wait for their instructions when we could go for a bath or when I could use it, because we were allowed only a certain amount of water during the day. They wouldn't let us use the gas all the time, you know. You had to cook quickly and just take your food away from the kitchen and then sit.

Because of our background, we would have been better off in East Africa, with my father's influence. My husband would be somewhere in parliament in politics; a good job, a nice house – a bungalow – where I didn't have to work, my children would have been spoilt by their grandparents. But as an individual I think we built up our confidence more here. Now I can survive in any country because that made us very strong.

GLORIA LESLIE
RETIRED NURSE AND CHARITY WORKER

Gloria is in the middle of cooking in the kitchen at the back of the restaurant. She is juggling serving customers and finishing up a pot soup in the kitchen. She then pulls out a pamphlet announcing the 15th Annual Charity Dinner and Dance at La Royale Banqueting Suite in Tottenham, her fundraiser to provide technical support for Noel Holmes Memorial Hospital and the Westhaven Children's Home in Jamaica to which she has devoted herself for the last eight years. She speaks about it with such kindness in her eyes. No self-aggrandisement, just passion to care.

The equipment, toys and other items are taken to Jamaica annually with the money raised at two major fundraising dinner and dance events, held in Tottenham. Both have become regular, much-anticipated events. She is also involved in the Jamaican Diaspora UK group which is run from the Jamaican Embassy in London.

For the younger generation it's a big change. Everyone is a mixture now! I had an Irish nanny for my child till she was 12 and she treat my child like it was her child! She had children of her own and her daughter had owned a really pretty bangle. When her girl finished with it she gave it to my daughter and now her daughter has it, so it's a tradition, a hand-me-down in our family. When my daughter had her children she would take them to visit Nanny. Through the end till Nanny died they had a good relationship.

I would say to the other nurses, 'Leave this one to me.' That one was mine. I would olive oil her skin to keep her nice. I didn't care what colour they were. I was here to do my job. I don't care you're old, you not going nowhere. Nurses of yesterday were caring people. Now they think of the money. There was a little white woman in Friern psychiatric hospital. People would complain she is making too much noise. Every night I would put a little brandy in her milk. I'm not joking. I kept that woman till she was 100 years old. I would dance and mess around. She would say 'Oh, look at her dance, that's vulgar, vulgar.'

I am a happy-go-lucky person. As far as prejudice goes, well you have to fit in. Maybe it's my personality, but it's not stopped me doing what I want to do. Basically, there is no way you are going to give in so they get used to you.

When you have an argument they would say, 'Go back to where you come from.' I would tease, 'Where to? Where I come from, the English even steal all the trees so I have no home to go back to!'

I show the kids traditional children's games like when we would play stones with the kids on the streets back in Jamaica, singing …

'Girl and boy going down Emmanuel Road. He fi broke rock stone, hit ye finger don't cry, gal and boy, Play we a play, break them one by one'.

It's really funny. It's a beautiful song.

← Gloria at her restaurant in Edmonton.

↑ West Indian nurses in Britain.

Connecting with the Locals

Kenneth working at St Pancras signalling office.

82　England Our England

KENNETH JEAN-MARIE
RETIRED SIGNALMAN

Teenage curiosity brought me to England. I wanted to get out and see what the other side was like.

It wasn't for economic reasons. I didn't really have preconceptions of the UK. I was very naive. In your desperation to leave the Caribbean island 27 miles long, you just wanted to get out. You didn't want to be like your parents. Looking back and seeing the ones who stayed and became school principals and so on with relative privileges and respect makes you wonder, but economically you are better off here than in St Lucia.

When I was a youngster here, we would play some cricket, not seriously though. We'd go to the pub and play darts. Some pubs wouldn't give you service but I never took it badly and didn't know if it was a colour thing or a class thing.

That's the difference between the first and second generations. They think they have a right to be here, but we knew we were foreigners.

We socialised with the other staff at St Pancras Station. There was no separation. Every six months we met in a place in Hertfordshire and had a social gathering where 99 per cent of the people were white. The area of work I was in had a few black people in it. We used to have what was called a bottle party. You would bring a bottle and invite your neighbours and so on, often to celebrate a graduation or christening.

I look back and have nothing to complain about, to be honest with you. I've never been out of work. I got trained up here at Signalling School and got a job straight away. The old-fashioned signal box was a small hut at the end of the platform. It has now been replaced with the lights controlled by people but not on the platform now. That's progress, not people getting in my way.

OVERLEAF A party with a mix of races enjoying themselves dancing.

I don't believe in a perfect world and in spite of Britain's history with slavery and so on I still consider it the best country on the planet. It is a very tolerant society on the whole, thinking about it.

CHAPTER FOUR

IDENTITY

*We would go clubbing a lot,
that's where we shone.*

DEREK BLAKE, RESTAURATEUR

CHAPTER FOUR

IDENTITY

FINDING OURSELVES

As subjects from the British colonies, many first-generation Indian and Afro-Caribbean people already had a sense of themselves as being part of Britain.

This sentiment, however, was not necessarily echoed by the British citizens, few of whom would have visited or had a close understanding of the cultural heritage, beliefs and values of the various groups of people in the British colonies at the time.

In the stories that we heard, there was evidence of a disconnect in the relationship between the British and newcomer communities; their sense of identity was different.

This chapter explores the sense of identity that immigrants experienced at a personal level. Moving to a different country – albeit the mother nation – is something that inevitably throws the issue of one's personal identity into stark relief: for a Sikh, for example, wearing a turban is an expected, habitual and therefore unnoticed thing, but it had now become a display drawing suspicion, scorn and unwanted attention. Why are the British so uptight and unfriendly, when all I am trying to do is enjoy the music? Why are they taking photographs of me; don't they understand they are stealing my soul? What does this say about who I am and who I should be or want to be?

Almost invariably, the people we talked to articulated or portrayed a great sense of pride in their homelands and heritage. Many steadfastly held on to their customs and rituals like a psychological anchor; some wanted to drop their old identity as fast as they could because they were embarrassed by their background; others were unsentimental about it and pragmatically let it go. For most, the move to Britain was a positive choice to advance in life rather than a rejection of where they came from.

This positivity is reflected in the fact that, over time, many Indian and Afro-Caribbean immigrants morphed into something else and began to define themselves as British. In particular, many seemed to embrace their host cities, places like London, Birmingham and Liverpool, as their own. There was also a sense of immigrants trying to cling to what they knew, but also finding, over time, that things felt foreign to them when they went home. In any case, by being in Britain and sometimes feeling rejected, immigrants often needed to go on quite a deep journey to find their identity.

Today, we see the lasting effects of immigration in many ways. It is not uncommon for British people to have mixed-race grandchildren, for example. Britain's own identity has also shifted over time. In sport, black people often compete for Great Britain and white British people identify with them.

What is it that makes someone British? I think the length of time you live in a country and the environment you are brought up in. My dad said to me, 'When in Rome, do as the Romans do.' So it's the manner of doing things, being part of the culture and a contributor to the culture. Deep down, I will never forget I am Jamaican.

DEREK BLAKE

← 'Gus' Osmond Philip's kitchen wall in Ladbroke Grove celebrating Malcom X.

'We are all in in it together' was the messaging for the war recruitment campaign for both world wars. After decades fighting the 'natives', the British discovered, with their backs to the wall, that they now needed soldiers from the Empire to help them survive. Over 1.3 million soldiers from India, 200,000 from African countries and even 15,000 from the tiny Caribbean were recruited to the effort in the First World War. Many served with distinction but their service was quickly forgotten. They were airbrushed out of history as the casual racism of the Empire returned with a vengeance. The Sikhs, who had been prominent in the war effort, were rewarded with the Jallianwala Bagh massacre at their holiest site, the Golden Temple in Amritsar, in 1919, the year after the war ended.

In the Second World War, the effort was even greater. Over 2.5 million Indians were enlisted into the effort as were hundreds of thousands of soldiers, merchant seamen and air force personnel from Africa and the Caribbean. By the time the war ended, the spell of Empire had been broken. The Americans forced a reluctant Britain to begin the process of relinquishing its colonies.

The call to work on transport and the NHS, to build a new Britain, was answered by people in the colonies. Those who had served the war effort were granted favourable immigration terms and many formed the early settler communities in Britain. In some places, the bonds of war helped. The Sikh community in Southall, for example, exists today because the owner of a rubber plant there, who had fond memories of fighting with Sikh soldiers, was one of the few to give the 'strange turbaned outsiders' employment. Elsewhere these early soldier migrants frequently found the welcome mat to be somewhat threadbare. The fight against the Germans and Japanese was replaced by a fight for acceptance in their new homes.

Beverley made a speech when she accepted her music doctorate saying she is proud to be female and proud to be British. The thing about it is that in Jamaica you grow up under the British Empire anyway. As I said, all the people in the government in Jamaica are British, all the exam papers are handed down from Britain and most of the things you learn are British anyway. We [British Commonwealth migrants to UK] all had British passports till 1962!

DELORIS SMITH

British public information poster.

Identity 91

I grew dreads back home after Brother Pinta gave a seminar about Marcus Garvey and Paul Bogle. These are our black heroes. School never taught me that. He said, read and learn about your history. The bookshop Grassroots was good fun, run by the Rasta. Grassroots is gone now. The police come and smash it up. There was a branch in every black neighbourhood. Basil Jarvis run it. Yeah, and my dressing changed a bit over after that. When I used to go to the West End and that, I used to trim my hair but when the Rasta come into it you go a bit more 'formal', you know – khaki and military, desert boots and ting! And you feel more relaxed and ting. The best thing that happened to me was being part of that movement. I have a whole wall full of vinyl from Bob Marley to Burning Spear. I'm setting things in motion to go back to the Caribbean now but I'd miss the mixture of people and the madness, oh and the red buses. Yeah, I lived three quarters of my life here so I guess I class myself as British. I was educated here. I am British. There are people back a yard who live better than me but they don't have enough experiences. UK is special. DARANCE LICORISH

← Daddy Vego, owner of People's Sound, arrived in Britain in the 1950s and set up the record shop along with a group of pioneers, now deceased, who championed reggae culture in Britain.

↑ Gus and Daddy Vego outside People's Sound, an institution and a home to the Rastafari movement in London, a celebration of the music and culture of Jamaican reggae music. At Carnival, the original People's Sound system would be directly outside his famous record shop.

Identity

NIC CAREEM
SOCIAL ENTREPRENEUR AND CONSERVATIVE CAMPAIGNER

I have been involved in politics all my life and have been a member of both Labour and then the Conservatives. I always felt that Labour was a hand-down not a hand-up mentality. However, I have not renewed my membership to the Conservative Party and now turn my interests entirely to working to end child poverty, homelessness and gang culture.

I have experienced more racism in the Labour Party than the Conservatives. I think that the Conservative Party, in the metropolis anyway, are much more enlightened. They have been to countries and so are much more accepting of different ways of life. They see things on merit basis only, which is what we want, not to be patronised. There are plenty of ethnic minorities that are there purely on ability. You see people that have uprooted their homes, generally are the kind of people that are pioneers, that tend to have Conservative values. You are going to work, you are going to make sacrifices; these are ingrained Conservative values.

When Ramen Bhattacharya was Mayor of Camden, he was the one who challenged Tony Blair to take him to the criminal war tribunal for the war in Iraq. He had this really Peter Sellers heavy Indian accent. I remember a very senior member of the local Hampstead Labour Party said to me, 'That man really irritates me. Why can't he speak English like the English? You know, like the Romans did.' I said, 'Oh, so wherever the Romans went they were like the local people too, weren't they? When the English went to Australia they were like the Aboriginals? When they went to America they smoked the peace pipe?' It's kind of a contradiction, 'when in Rome'. It doesn't happen the other way round.

It's illegal to call someone a 'black bastard' but not to call someone a bitch or an idiot. Sometimes you can be ignorant through no fault of your own. I don't want to discriminate against ignorance. My friend John Bird is a prime example of this. Up to the age of 15 he couldn't read or write and was a right racist. He is now Britain's number one social entrepreneur. He has an amazing intellect. His knowledge of art is phenomenal, completely self-educated.

This brings me to the Eva Schloss Anne Frank play we tour in prisons. Where we train prisoners to take a job as a guide, we give them a proper ceremony and certificate. They have never been given anything in their lives. The look on their faces is fantastic. With this work the rehabilitation rate is much higher than the norm. If you don't value yourself, you don't value anyone else. Give the prisoners self-esteem.

I took the play to Pentonville and the Muslim prisoners who came up to Eva and the other Holocaust survivors who were there were unbelievably supportive. We knew some of the prisoners were killers. We weren't asking where they had come from; we are interested in where they are going. The point is: whoever we are, we can change our future.

I brought Trevor Philips along because he was interested in getting the Labour mayoralty in 2000. Two Labourites came up to me and said London would never elect a black mayor. I said, 'No, you are wrong about that, I believe if you can do the job, you will be elected regardless of colour.'

← Nic with three of his four children. The eldest girl is now BBC South Asia Bureaux Chief. The middle daughter is a senior NHS manager and the boy is a successful technology entrepreneur.

↑ Nic (holding baby on the right) with his family.

↓ Nic with his daughter Nicola, now BBC South Asia News Bureaux Chief.

→ Conservative Party supporters at the Conservative Party Conference, Brighton, 1976.

This is what I have learnt going into prisons – some prisoners have been the most incredibly intelligent people I have met. I want to tour a play with a prisoner, a rehabilitee hit man. The play would stop half way to give the audience a chance to consider different options he should take, for instance to see what would come of his life through being given an education. This is part fiction but the protagonist's dilemma is a real-life one. Had his talents been nurtured, he could have been anybody and he is living proof of this.

You see people that have uprooted their homes generally are the kind of people that are pioneers, that tend to have Conservative values. You are going to work, you are going to make sacrifices; these are ingrained Conservative values.

I remember a very senior member of the local Hampstead Labour Party said to me, 'That man really irritates me, why can't he speak English like the English? You know, like the Romans did.' I said 'Oh, so wherever the Romans went they were like the local people too, weren't they? When the English went to Australia they were like the Aboriginals? When they went to America, they smoked the peace pipe? It's kind of a contradiction, 'when in Rome.' It doesn't happen the other way round.

Identity

It was hard to get any half-decent job and we would go out every day knocking on factory doors. We all got lots of rejections. One day, without telling anyone I went to the bathroom and cut my hair and took my turban off. I slipped out to look for work hoping the others would not see me. That day, I got my first half-decent job as a signalman at the railways. When I got home the other Sikh men said, 'Piara Singh, what have you done?'

↑ Piara Singh Bains in his first job as a railway worker.

↑ Piara Singh Bains posing for a photograph to be sent back to his family in India.

PIARA SINGH BAINS
COLLEGE PRINCIPAL, RAILWAY SIGNALMAN AND POST OFFICE WORKER

After my marriage in India on 31 January 1951, my wife and I had three children, two girls and a boy. I worked as a teacher in Physics, Chemistry and English, and, I was promoted at the age of 32 to be the headmaster of the Khalsa High School. I became well known in the area and Congress wanted me to run for parliament. However, I also wanted to improve the quality of life for my family. This, as well as my love for English literature, made me try to move to England.

On arrival in England in 1962, I went to the Ilford area as this was where the only Sikh I knew in the country lived. I settled in with a group of Sikh men in a house in the area. They knew me by reputation and called me 'Masterji' because of my job back home.

I looked for professional jobs with Plessey and also teaching posts but it was difficult as my degree was not really recognised in England.

It was hard to get any half-decent job and we would go out every day knocking on factory doors. We all got lots of rejections. One day, without telling anyone I went to the bathroom and cut my hair and took my turban off. I slipped out to look for work hoping the others would not see me. That day, I got my first half-decent job as a signalman at the railways. When I got home the other Sikh men said, 'Piara Singh, what have you done?'

The work was hard and involved looking after and repairing the signal lights along the tracks between London and Suffolk. Most of the work was done at night and usually it was extremely cold. I had never seen snow before and remember the cold flakes falling from the night sky one evening and shivering with amazement and shock! I worked at nights and undertook overtime whenever possible. The men I lived with took turns to cook and, being one of the most educated and fluent in English, I spent much of my time helping complete job application forms. I worked hard and saved all that was possible. I sent my family regular letters, telegrams and spare money. I tried not to think too much about missing loved ones in Punjab but the thought of my children growing up and not being there to see, hear or be with them was becoming increasingly difficult to bear. Eventually, with help from another Sikh, I brought a house. I was one of the first to own one. I raised money to pay back my friend, and for my wife and children's travel expenses to come over from India.

I intentionally wore a suit and bowler hat as a way of introducing my family to the new me, and to the English culture, when I went to meet them at Dover in 1963. They barely recognised me without my turban and beard but it was a joyous reunion.

At home we all initially had to sleep in one room because the lodgers occupied the other rooms. Together we went to the local shops to buy food, winter clothes and school uniforms for the children. We had no car so we had to walk to and from places and carry the entire goods home. My wife and I had clear roles and responsibilities. I largely concentrated on the finances and settling the children into the local schools and teaching them English. I continued to work nights and undertake as much overtime as possible. Within two years all three of our children were accepted into the local grammar schools. Once we could afford not to have lodgers, my wife and I had a further three children, two girls and a boy.

I left the railway and accepted a 'sorting' position working for the Post Office. I continued to work nights and fortunately had enough money to pay a short visit to my mother, who was ill in India. After a few years, I received a letter saying my mother had died. It was such a sad way to find out and I went to a room to be by myself.

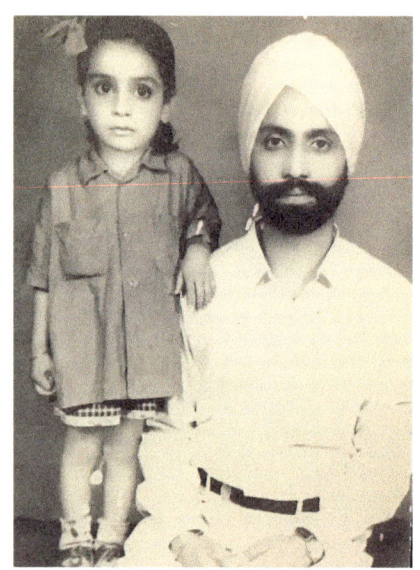

I had no strong desire to return to India after that.

We didn't have enough money to go on holidays but took day trips to the seaside when possible or visited friends or relatives. I have to say the financial demands were endless but my wife and I saved enough for a car and a bigger house in the same area. Any remaining money was put aside for the children's future or to lend to other relatives or friends who needed help. Hard as my life was, I did not regret the decision to migrate. While I would have been better off in India perhaps, my children all got degrees and good jobs in the UK. We felt our sacrifices were worth it.

The emotional strain and upset was greater as the children became older and moved from home to go to universities. It became apparent that aspects of Indian culture and values that my wife and I had grown up with were challenging for them. My wife and I tried to understand and our views on these issues also changed with time and we allowed our children to make their own choices. Many of my close relatives and friends relied on my advice and support but it became apparent that they only understood my approach once they and their families started to have the same issues to deal with.

I also felt responsible for protecting my family from hostility from the host culture. I remember clearly in 1975 when my wife and I received death threats from people in a neighbourhood where we were about to buy a house. In the end we bought another, better place nearby but not before the neighbours were asked whether they 'minded having Indians living near them'.

I didn't pay as much attention to my diet and physical health as perhaps I should have. My life was hard and busy. The mental and physical pressure took its toll in my sixties when I started to suffer from heart problems followed by a major stroke. I had to retire from work soon afterwards.

When I look back, I can see how my ambition to move to this country has been fulfilled in a sense through my children. I am proud of all of them for their educational and career achievements as well as settling and adapting to life in this country so well. In particular, I can see my adventurous spirit in my eldest daughter who has successfully established a life and career for herself and her family in California. My eldest son aspired to high educational and career achievements and successfully obtained a PhD from Oxford University and has set up his own business. The other children are also doing well.

I was always someone who pushed forward. I was the first to get a degree in my area and one of the first to come to England. I was one of the first to buy a house and also to allow my children more freedom than others felt able to give. I see this spirit in my wife and my children.

← Piara visiting his relatives in the Punjab.

← With his son Gurnek.

↓ This certificate shows how many people like Piara were forced to take jobs far below their capabilities.

I intentionally wore a suit and bowler hat as a way of introducing my family to the new me, and to the English culture, when I went to meet them at Dover in 1963. They barely recognised me without my turban and beard but it was a joyous reunion.

School Motto :- Love, Service & Sacrifice.

From
The Headmaster
J. S. F. H. KHALSA HIGH SCHOOL
(Chak No. 73 R. B.)
NAWANSHAHR DOABA (*Jullundur*)

To

No _____   Dated 3 - 7 - 196 1

It gives me an immense pleasure to certify that S.Piara Singh B.Sc.,B.T. at present Headmaster, joined this school on 30.6.1955 as a Senior Science Teacher. He has perfect mastery over Science and can teach English and Maths. with equal efficiency to the high classes.

His most excellent results in the Matriculation Examination during the last 5 years speak for themselves as to his efficiency, devotion to duty and painstaking habits. His becoming the Head of such a big institution at the age of 33 years is a testimony in itself to his great qualities of both head and heart. The institution is forging ahead in all diverse fields of education e.g. instruction, games and extra-mural activities. He has tone toned up the discipline of the school considerably.

He has about 9 years' teaching experience in well-established and big recognised High Schools and has been examiner in Science in the Matriculation Examination of the Panjab University for the last so many years.

He bears a very high moral character and is, indeed, an asset for this school.

I wish him all luck in his life.

Chanan Singh
Manager
J.S.F.H. KHALSA HIGH SCHOOL,
NAWA SHAHAR (Jullundur).

Identity 101

ELOUISE EDWARDS MBE
COMMUNITY ACTIVIST

Stepping into Elouise's house you cannot help but be overwhelmed by the collections that her house is decorated with; an assortment of trinkets, mementos and souvenirs as well as bookshelves stacked with books, a single-minded theme: the improvement of society and particularly the people of the Black Diaspora. Then there is the bordering-on-obsessive Egyptomania theme that adorns the walls and a stained-glass tableaux front-door surround. There's an unusual portrait of Jesus Christ as a black man, countless images of joyful black children and dolls in various cultural costume. 'Years ago I bought a black baby doll at Brixton market and I called him Little Willie. I said to the local supermarket, "Why have you only got white dolls? Look at your clientele – there is a majority percentage of black residents!"'

I came in 1961 from Guyana by plane and ship when I was 28. I followed my husband a year after he came to study and practise lithography here in Manchester. He designed handkerchief boxes and every box you could think of. The company was called Stevenson's Box Works. He was very good, the youngest foreman there. I have four sons. Even though I am retired there are things I am involved with now. There is a huge driving force. I'm also driven by hard work and my thoughts, very positive thoughts.

I began life here working at the hotel Manchester Piccadilly. I met up with a lot of people from all over the world. They wanted all kinds of things done through me. I had been to school and had qualifications so could assist them in their paperwork, applications, that sort of thing.

I have set up many businesses catering for the black community here. There was so much lacking. The African Caribbean Mental Health Service was the first one that we worked with. There was a doctor there who was a close associate of mine. We applied for some money and we got it. Our greatest achievement in housing provision is Bougainvillea Gardens and we just had our 25th anniversary celebration. The first person to be re-housed had sickle cell. We set up the community initiative housing trust Abisinde because the police were harassing black males and this place would be a refuge for us to attend to them. We would look after all people though I remember a time when we took in a young white lad, who had been beaten by the police so badly, when we saw his blood like rain falling. He turned to me and said, 'And to think you are the people we were taught to hate.'

When night comes, you see that lamp post on the corner, there the little boys are on the bikes selling drugs. It breaks my heart. If people open their eyes they will see that the powers that be are out to get rid of us because they think that one day we will retaliate against what they have done to us in the past and they are scared. They can't see that we go to war with ourselves but generally have been peaceful people.

↑ Elouise was awarded an MBE for her work in 1994 for services to the community in Manchester.

→ Elouise at her house in Moss Side.

When my husband died we set up a library in his honour. It is a reference library dedicated to people of African descent. It's called Nana Bonsu Library, as that was his title. My husband would lecture at that university. He grew up in that kind of background, getting acquainted with his history. He used to run the West Indian Centre and if you ask around about Beresford Edwards they will say, 'Oh yes, that big tall man.'

I class myself as an African born in South America, Guyana. I use the British passport because it gives me freedom to move but when I see so much prejudice still going on I do not want to align myself with that.

The youngsters think they are British but they don't know what the British really think of them. The kids and the world looking out upon them see criminality as part of them.

My husband always said, 'Not knowing is ignorance but not wanting to know is a criminal offence.' With reference to the ancient civilisation of Egypt, they should know that we have been uplifted long before anyone else.

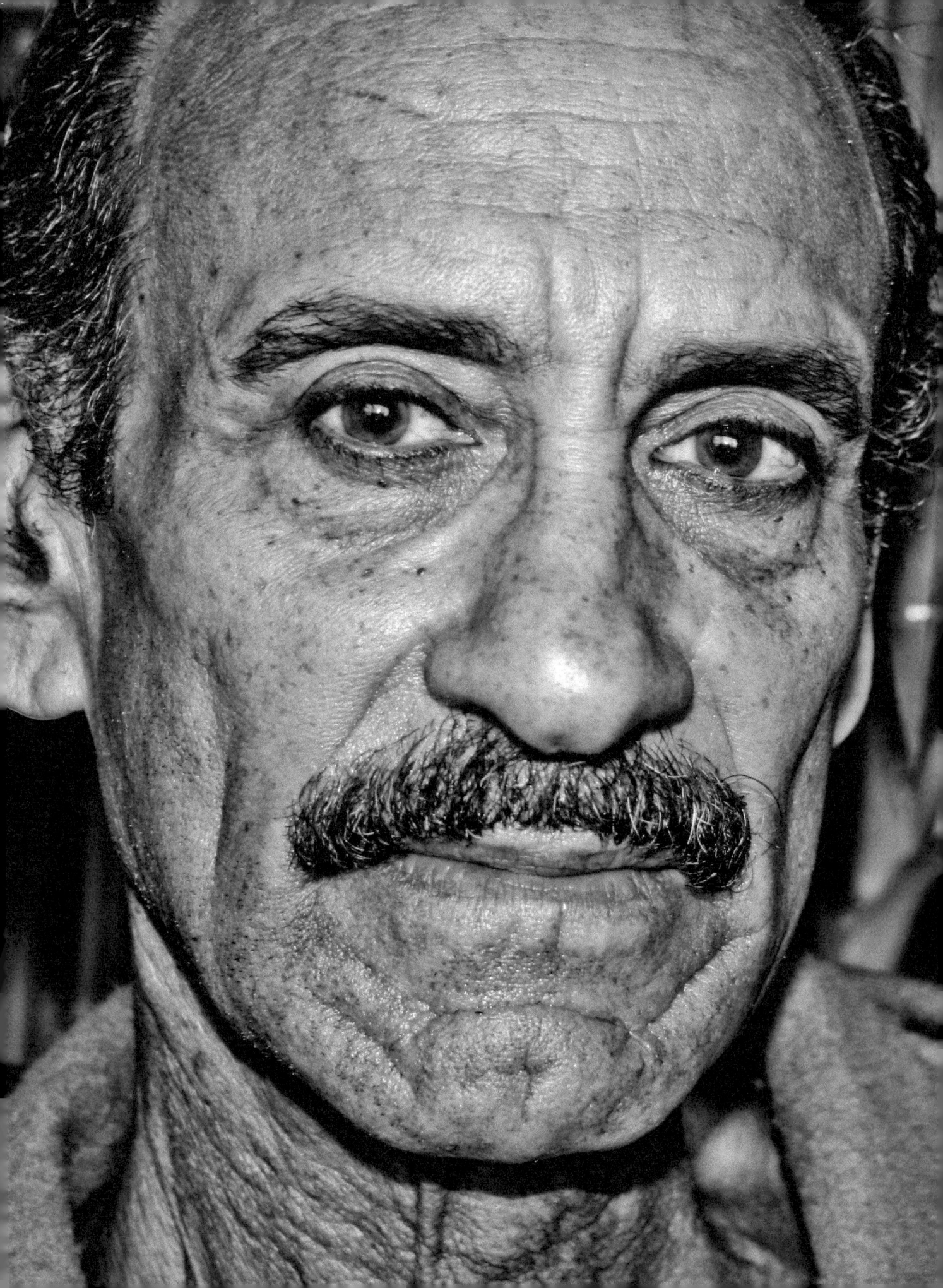

STEFAN KALIPHA
ACTOR AND BUDDHIST ELDER

We come from a middle-class family in Trinidad. My uncles and my grandfather were merchants; they had businesses.

There is a big emphasis on colour shades and class which has been a blight on West Indian culture, but we were not a closed middle-class family, I think because of Carnival we have stayed open. We lived in a working-class area, a famous place in Trinidad, right next to the big bands like Renegade Steel Band. When I came here I was one of ten players in one of the first steel bands, which made up the carnival here in London. We would end up playing parties for the Queen.

I would hang out with my cousin Horace Ové. He always had a lot of front and my nature was more trusting and open. He used to say, 'Why you stupid, you always so honest and apologising.' Now, with my Buddhist study I realise it's OK, I was on the right track.

When I first came to London at 19 in the early '60s, I lived in a house with a guy called Stirling Bedako who had a band called TSPO (Trinidad Steel Percussion Orchestra) and an English guy, John Lindon, who was a very political animal and taught me about organic food and a hell of a lot about politics, world affairs and metaphysics. We partied a lot. They were very exciting times with the Black Power movement and Michael X and I was in the middle of it all, always questioning things.

I was always interested in what is the truth, what is reality. I found some people were just promoting themselves really. I saw through the hypocrisy of some of it, so much so that Michael X told Horace not to bring his cousin (me) back in his house. Michael X from Trinidad, he was a strong leader in that movement and Peter Carmichael also. Darcus Howe also had very strong political views. I knew what was going on. I heard a lot of dialogue going on. People were trying to make something of their lives and trying to promote black consciousness, which was good.

People were looking at Black Power politics and I wanted to go deeper. I started to read about Buddhism. I then got interested in a group of wonderful people involved in esoteric Christianity. In 1983 I spent a good deal of time back in Trinidad. It was incredible, this beautiful island I had come from and all these beautiful girls of every colour and shape you can think of. I came back to a grey, cold day in London and the contrast to the noise, colour, physical access to Maracas Beach and the parties made me totally depressed. But an American actress called Sheila Scott Wilkinson who was in Horace's film *Pressure* talked to me about Buddhism and everything she said resonated with what I have always felt, so I started chanting and practising Buddhism.

I used to be the head of the Soca Gakkai, which was a group for Afro-Caribbeans, recognising the particular things to discuss on racial oppression. Now I work with my Buddhist Centre as a Chapter Leader, where we teach all to be free within themselves.

The human race originated from a small amount of people in Africa. Therefore everyone is your brother. You start to realise that everyone is connected.

In Buddhism they say there are three kinds of people, ones that moan, one who don't say much either way and another that makes you feel good. I hope to be that one, who makes you feel your life is worth living.

↑ Stefan with his daughter.

Moss Side, Manchester, 1972.

CHAPTER FIVE

COMMUNITIES LOST AND FOUND

We were a community. Us black people were more loving with each other. Come Christmas, we didn't have phone and all that, you would just turn up.
DOROTHY YOUNG

Vijay Dhir's evidence of a Christmas Eve attack on his home by the National Front.

CHAPTER FIVE

COMMUNITIES LOST AND FOUND

CONNECTIONS IN A STRANGE WORLD

The migrant households of the 1960s were characteristically communal which, at least at that time, was very different from the British way.

The communities that migrants had left behind might have been lost to them, but they found and carved out new ones. United as newcomers, migrants were inevitably drawn together: to others who looked and sounded like them; and to people who were experiencing the same stresses and shocks in transitioning into a new and strange world. Through daily interaction, the creation of spiritual worship, debating current affairs from home and social groups like blues parties, they gradually built a sense of belonging.

Inevitably, migrants settled into areas where rental and housing prices were most affordable. Relatives and friends coming to Britain would most often join them in the same areas and hence newcomer communities grew. Friendships were formed, favours were traded, sons and daughters married, creating a tapestry of memories, trust and wonderful stories of kinship.

Familiarity in the midst of the unknown is always comforting and it is possible that the nature of their situation pulled together migrant people who would not normally have connected or even associated in their home countries. Indeed, Indians and Afro-Caribbeans were originally much softer with each other and helped each other out more in the early days of settling into Britain, when they were few, than they necessarily do nowadays.

That said, migrants also established a sense of community with white British people where they integrated and morphed in various ways with them. Early notions of 'togetherness' and neighbourly connection were created between the Caribbean and British populations, for example, in Ladbroke Grove in London. At that time, it could be argued that both were relatively against the Moroccans who were perceived as being out for themselves and not assimilating or contributing to the broader social fabric.

Polarities in the way that Afro-Caribbean and Indian migrant groups established a sense of community in Britain have, in many ways, shaped the structure of things as we see them today. For example, attitudes to investing in property were different from the outset: the objective for many Caribbeans was to spend just a few years working in Britain before going back to buy property and settle long-term in their sunny homeland. In contrast, Indians more collectively perceived the move to Britain as permanent and therefore sought to gain a strategic foothold in the country, either in the form of housing or business enterprises, like corner shops and restaurants. Consequently, Indians tended to set up mortgages early on and held on to property. Over time, this has inevitably led to some clear distinctions in prosperity between the two groups today.

We formed our own community. It didn't matter which part of Punjab anyone came from, we were all one Punjabi family. We helped each other with money so that no one was in debt. Those were the good old days, simply because we all survived through our hard work.

VIJAY DHIR, PHOTOGRAPHER

↓ Dorothy Young outside her house in Harvist Road, Kensal Rise.

→ A woman walks past Silchester Road in the Notting Hill area of London after its demolition to make way for the Westway flyover, 1967.

In the early 1960s Southall was said to have five Indian food shops; by the late 1970s the Asian community of 15,000 was served by a variety of businesses. It could not be said that the immigrant population was lacking in initiative or failing to contribute economically.

Nevertheless, home ownership for many migrants in the 1960s and 70s became a matter of survival, if not always an explicit aspiration. The now infamous posters, 'No blacks, No Irish, No dogs', could be seen all too frequently on the front doors of private landlord properties and sadly symbolised the reason for this necessity. The private rental market was then unregulated, thus giving way to blatant discrimination, and landlords often ruthlessly exploited desperate migrants with high rents and terrible conditions.

A practice known as 'partners', brought over from the Caribbean, was a popular way for people to pool their funds in order to achieve group ownership of property.

Things changed over time and several factors contributed to the lack of Caribbeans owning homes in Britain. Firstly, those who sold up, moved back home and eventually decided to return to Britain, frequently found it difficult to re-enter the housing market. Secondly, property rises and the boom of development in central city areas across the country in the late 1970s often enticed homeowners to sell up, to their eventual detriment. Thirdly, 'buy out' schemes and the government's offer to re-house people in new, modern council flats was an appealing short-term proposition but not, as it turned out, a wise strategic move.

Residents of Moss Side in Manchester had the same fate as those in parts of Notting Hill. They remember the sprawling estate as a friendly community of West Indians and British living side by side, but again communities were 'bought out' in the name of development. Here, they lost the sense of neighbourhood cohesiveness because the dispersion led to an erosion of trust and support for each other. Moss Side resident Elouise Edwards remembers shops that would serve and support the Caribbean residents including selling hard-to-come-by black dolls before the regeneration occurred.

What is not well known is that, in the two decades that followed the arrival of the Empire Windrush, *rates of home ownership among Afro-Caribbean and other new Commonwealth migrants actually exceeded those of the white English population in Britain.*

Council regeneration and gentrification projects meant that whole estates were sometimes knocked down, streets were chopped in half and predominantly black neighbourhoods were turned into building sites, for example with the construction of the Westway through North Kensington in London.

THE ENTERPRISE

There is a new thing happening and the media haven't yet caught on but here is a fusion between the black church and the Chinese church. The black church is very vibrant in terms of its worship and its colour whereas the Chinese are business people with their own shops but pretty bound-in emotionally. So, you put the two together and it's whoosh! Yes, it is a British institution injected with a new lease of life by the immigrant population.

LORD TAYLOR OF WARWICK

← Bar in London, 1975.

← Pentecostal church in London, 1978.

→ Makeshift Gurdwara in Southall, 1978.

→ Waiting to go on an outing outside Top Rank Bowling Alley, Southall, 1960.

Communities Lost and Found

The corner shop could be seen as an everyday 'contact zone', defined by cultural theorist Mary Louise Pratt as 'social spaces where disparate cultures meet, clash and grapple with each other'. This 'contact zone' is one in which 'native' and 'settler' interact in seemingly banal ways that may nonetheless be fraught with the tensions and connections that characterise multicultural Britain.

The shopkeeper's role came to the forefront recently in the Covid-19 pandemic and as a nation we thanked our key workers for keeping us sustained in groceries, deliveries, and of course healthcare. The fact that these key workers were predominantly of foreign origin exemplifies our multi-ethnic cohesiveness and the 'all in it together' spirit of British society in a time of crisis.

By the 1950s Indian-owned grocery shops and later hair-product shops were specifically patronised by black customers. So there was a time in Britain when black people were the only shoppers who would use Asian businesses. They were so happy to have the produce from the tropics that they knew and loved, such as yams and dried salt fish.

By the 1960s, with an increase in travel to exotic destinations and the quest to be more open to the romantic aspect of Indian culture, nag champa and curry powder had suddenly become essential to white Britain, and 'foreign shopkeepers' were becoming more socially acceptable.

Sadly, these shopkeepers face much racial prejudice on the front line and serving the community at large and do so to this day: recently Indian workers at a Hampstead branch of Tesco were subjected to racial abuse by drunken youths. The difference is that today that abuse is finally taken seriously and the offenders were taken to court.

↑ An Indian couple serving a customer at their grocery shop, 1955.

OVERLEAF Shopkeeper Komor Uddin serves a customer at the Taj Stores in Brick Lane, East London, 1978.

Communities Lost and Found   117

VIJAY DHIR
RAILWAY PORTER, PHOTOGRAPHER

I arrived in the UK in March 1962. On arrival I found this place very quiet and lonely.

I stayed with my uncle who had been living here since 1957. After a couple of months I found a job at Paddington Station as a railway porter. Indians were not easily considered for clerical or other office positions as there was a notion that all immigrants were only fit for menial jobs. The first months were very difficult periods, as it was more of a shame to work as a porter, but there was no choice. That sort of feeling was common among all of us. But the job of a porter took me to my destination. Within eight months, I passed the railway clerical exams and became a full-time clerk. The whole office welcomed me with respect. I met some very nice people. I was the youngest person among 150 office staff.

I was always interested in photography and the chief engineer of the railway helped me to get a job as a film cameraman for British Transport Films. I was only 19 years old and was possibly one of the very luckiest Indians at that time.

I then worked a full ten years within the railway framework and thoroughly enjoyed every day of my life. I was never looked down on as an Indian. I was always at the forefront with other members. I played a very active role organising office outings. I went around the UK and Europe with English friends many times on holiday. I was now a senior cameraman at Marylebone head office of British Transport Films.

During the days of portership there was shift work. At night during a break, everyone would go to the cafeterias but I would find a quiet place in an isolated corner to lay on a bench, facing the wall and I would cry my head out. This happened every night over a long period. I missed my parents very badly.

At the beginning, life was sad and quiet and I was homesick, missing my family.

Back in Southall, where I lived, things were not too bad. We were all men or very young boys. About 12–14 people lived in one house at a time as there was no other accommodation available. We all had rolling bedding so that everyone had a personal bed, but we all slept on the floor. We cooked together and ate together, sitting on the floor sharing one bowl of dal and picking up chapatis by hand. It was like sharing a langar food at a Gurdwara. We would all go to the pub in the evening but dare not go to any London clubs as we would be looked down on as 'blacks' or 'wogs'. These words of insult were very common in those days. We all got used to this abuse and learnt how to swallow our pride and never looked for trouble. In reality, that was our strength.

Sometimes we would stay all night celebrating something silly; dancing, singing film songs, singing qawwalis and finally crying. This used to be a cry of joy and loneliness, not of any sadness. We formed our own community. It didn't matter which part of Punjab anyone came from, we were all one Punjabi family. We helped each other with money so that no one was in debt. Those were the good old days, simply because we all survived through our hard work.

I regularly wrote letters home and sent photographs of London and myself. My father was my best friend and wrote letters with up-to-date information about the Punjab and my family.

My mother also wrote to me regularly. Her letters were of a different kind.

At the beginning, life was sad and quiet and I was homesick, missing my family.

← Vijay at Paddington Station.

Every letter used to have tear marks, tear drops all over her letters; I could smell the tears. Every word I read was as if she was talking to me. That used to be a whole day reserved for crying.

After the railways, I worked at County Hall, with the Greater London Council (GLC) as a senior press photographer. The press office was also responsible to the Royal Commission which was directly linked to the Royal Family's press affairs. I was commissioned to photograph the Queen Mother for a portrait to celebrate her 80th birthday. A happy picture won me the 'Highest Award'. The Royal Commission titled the photograph 'The Spirit of London' and I won the Best Photographer of the Year award. This photograph became an icon for London and had numerous publications. It was exhibited at the Royal Festival Hall for one month for public viewing. I received a personal letter from the Queen Mother's office to say how delighted she was with my photograph.

During my stay with the GLC till 1986, I had the pleasure to photograph very important people, from Oscar-winning film stars to presidents. I felt very privileged to photograph all members of the Royal Family over and over. It was a great honour to be in the company of Her Majesty many times, sometimes one-to-one.

Now I decided to take a post at Central Saint Martins as a photographer in the Media Services department to photograph all college events and students' work for present and future publications. I was asked to form a team of strong technicians to provide advanced services to the college network, and I was appointed Head of Media Services. This area was very important to the college and my job changed from practical to administrative work.

The so-called National Front made our life very difficult. This happened in February 1982. The swastika

Every letter used to have tear marks, tear drops all over her letters; I could smell the tears. Every word I read was as if she was talking to me. That used to be a whole day reserved for crying.

would be written on our cars and notices such as 'Get out now or else' were put under our car wipers. The police were not helpful at all. I was told to forget all about it, these things do happen. There was no help.

One night in December 1984 at about 3am we heard a very loud bang from downstairs in our house. To our shock the front-room windows were smashed; a few bricks and a large piece of stone with some metal attached had been thrown through the glass. We were frightened and shocked, just thinking, what next? My young children were shivering and crying. Some neighbours came out to help and comfort us. We were under the impression that we were very much liked in the area where we lived. They were all trying to assure us that they hadn't been responsible for the incident. I called the police and got the same sort of unhelpful response as the first time. The slogans of the National Front were painted on our car.

Then one night in February 1985, hell came down on us. At about midnight they came back; about four or five of them in total. It was like a terrorist attack! They threw red bricks and stones; not a window in the house was spared. Luckily no one was hurt. At that point, I felt it was no good to call the police, though I did make a 999 call. Two policemen turned up but as soon as I mentioned the National Front, they became angry with me so I told them to get out of the house!

← Vijay as a young porter.

← Vijay as a railway photographer.

↑ With the Mayor of Uxbridge at the opening ceremony of the Queen's Diamond Jubilee Exhibition, 2012.

↑ *The Mirror* features Vijay as the photographer of The Queen Mother.

Communities Lost and Found 123

Vijay Dhir's photo evidence of the vandalism to his car and threats to his home by the National Front.

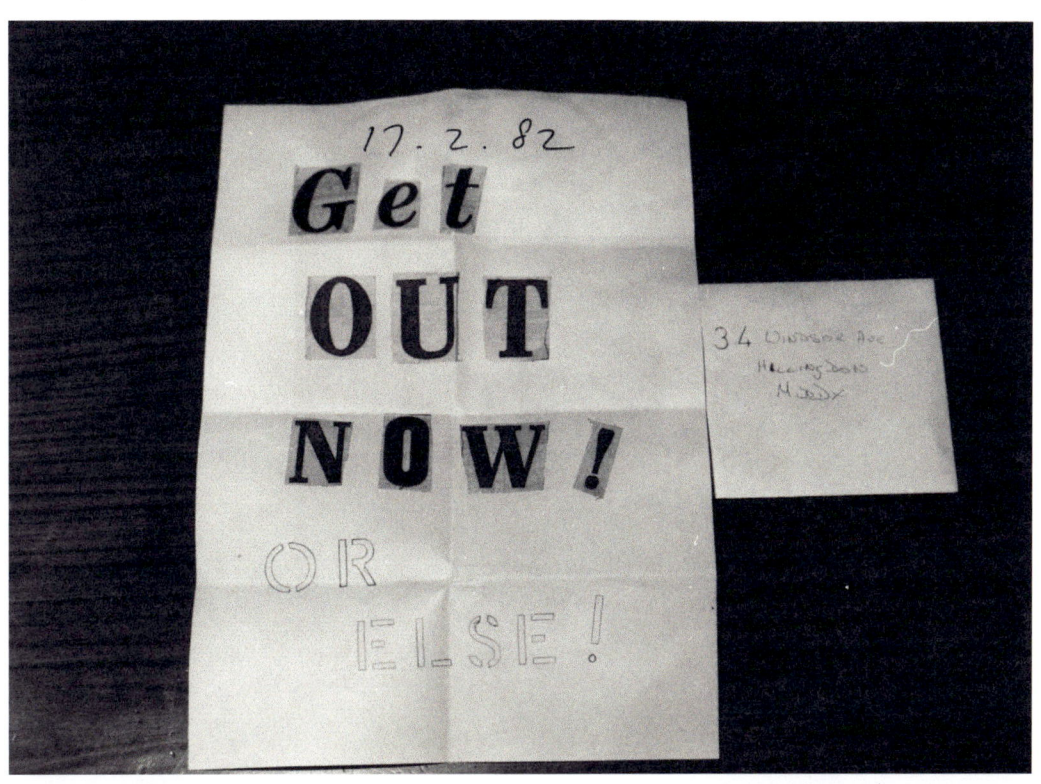

Communities Lost and Found 125

DARANCE LICORISH
FULL-TIME FATHER

Darance sits outside a café off the Golborne Road and tells of life in 'The Grove', (Ladbroke Grove). His life here is like a yarn spun and held together by the various threads of a strong community. However, since coming here in 1963 when he was just 12 years old, Darance feels the provisions for black youths and community hangouts in the area have slowly been taken away.

Just giving an insight into the Grove, the early days man, what a big change, eh. Yeah, tell me about it, the Grove man. The guys two, three years older than me – Frank Sweeny an' them older guys, if we were to go to a club in Shepherd's Bush or Harlesden, we would have the guys behind us. They would not let anyone beat us up. Nice. You have grown up together.

The Metro, on the corner of Tavistock and St Luke's Road, it's now flats or something. Sad. We grew up in that place. Friday, Saturday you could go play table tennis, pool football; proper youth club. It all got lost. Artists would come from Jamaica; Alton Ellis, The Mighty Diamonds, them guys come play there!

There was an incident where somebody died. So the police closed it down in the early '80s. People would come from as far as Liverpool, Manchester. Tabernacle (the mainstay community centre here) don't carry the same weight. Metro was our thing.

I was in my 20s then. Used to go to the West End, come back here and then go Metro. Used to go to all the clubs. Flamingos, The Attires, Whisky-A-Go-Go, see Georgie Fame and all those guys. Would be wearing bell-bottom trousers; it was the '60s, really fun. Everything was changing, all colours mixed in, Flower Power time, hippies and all that, nice! When the music come in, you don't find that foolishness, race thing. They free up themselves. No fear.

In those days, them guys around here that are like 70 something now, 15 years or so older than me, like Sunny, were really dressed up. They would come out after having had their bath and dress up. I remember Mr Baker with his cream suit, cream hat on, walking down the road. The white guys would look on and say, 'Who is this? Is he famous?' He was just Mr Baker. Two of them characters, one named Parachute, he owns Crazy Clothes Connection. He's still there now. He had a big white American car like a plane flying 'Scwhhhh'. You could hear it before you saw it. Flamboyant!

Mostly men come first from the Caribbean to check it out then send for their lady.

Likkle Miss, wife of Sledge, big tall guy, tough, dreadlocks thick and white, looked like Moses ta Rass! He died in a fire last year. They were the King and the Duchess. When they go party he is wearing Crimplene and she is wearing worsted mohair suit. If it's blue tonight or green tomorrow they're the same, was wicked. They were the characters.

Then there was Lord Cloak, top Socca artist. People see him and don't know nothing about him. The best sound was Duke Vin, so we follow that sound wherever it goes, Birmingham, Manchester, wherever.

School was easy. We had English class back in the Caribbean. White kids were not listening to the teachers, jumping on the desks, spitting at each other. I thought, 'You mad! If you try that back home, you dead! You would get the most beatings!' Caribbean boys never joined into that foolishness. School was all right. I liked

← Portobello Road Market, London, late 1950s.

the dinner! Yeah, I mixed with the white kids. Some of them bare foolishness. But I remember my friend Charlie Matthews, a white guy. He was labelled a 'dunce' and he used to copy me. I would tell him to go away. The Caribbean guys were much brighter and I am not being racist. They were more disciplined.

I remember one teacher, Mr Turnbull with his big voice and thick leather belt. But he was a nice guy. Voice like thunder. We would just keep quiet. The deputy head wore the same pants for years till they had a shine on them like a mirror!

The guys in the store up there, I know the whole family, the boys took over the business. He said, 'Hey Darance, you know what, I liked it when it was just you lot only. Bloody Moroccans.'

I said, 'Yeah, but you didn't like us when we first came!' The Moroccans up there said something to me about running the place. I said you better shut up. If you had come when I came they would have kicked your ass. Boy when we came we had to fight for our lives, boy. We set things up.

When Frank Critchlow owned nearly all of All Saints Road, the police did not like it! They hated him. They had a dartboard in the police station with his face as a target. They tried to frame him. Arrested him, took him to the station and threw him on the floor. The police planted drugs on him and then filmed them taking the drugs out of his pocket. He had a good lawyer who showed that the camera was stopped and started where they said they had filmed it all in one go. It also helped that Frank's best friend happened to be the local Conservative MP for Kensington and Chelsea!

They did not want to see black people owning anything, man. The problem was the cops. They were a headache! One of the cops said to me, 'I dreaded the day when I saw you.' One called Edwards; I used to give him hell. I said, 'You don't like me and I don't like you either. I live here, you only come and work here.' I said, off the record, 'Let's go round the back and see what happens to you. If they try to nick me, we gonna have a fight 'cause I haven't done nothing!'

← All Saints Road in Notting Hill was the backdrop to much action in the community from the Christine Keeler affair to the Mangrove.

↓ Community centre in Wolverhampton, 1978.

OVERLEAF The Four Aces Club on Dalston Lane in Hackney was a popular spot for West Indian men to dance and mingle.

Communities Lost and Found   129

Mustapha in front of Trinidadian masks.

MUSTAPHA MATURA
(1939–2019)
PLAYWRIGHT

I was 20 when I came here. I was working as a clerk at the Docks – nice job, very casual though. When I first arrived, I stayed with a friend in Earl's Court. He was doing mail order fraud, great character. He was a big, jolly guy and a natural hustler, a child of his time really. Before he came to London he orchestrated this Sam Cook scam, saying he was getting him over to play. People bought tickets for a gig that never materialised. Then he got people to sign up to come to his 'modelling school'. It was very successful, all the Trini girls wanted to be models. One Indian family did not have the money to pay for their daughter so gave him a cow. When his time was up and justice came for him some people came to his house and looked through the keyhole. All they could see was an empty room with a cow standing there.

I got a job in the Euston Road at the National Temperance Hospital as a porter. That was the start of my London life. I was hanging out with Horace Ové who is a film director now. We were all into the arts and modern things. We were all feeding off each other and bouncing ideas, stimulating a creative environment to express ourselves. At weekends we would listen to calypso and jazz and visit a cinema in Tottenham Court Road to see the latest French films, which was really great exposure for me to an alternative culture.

Horace and I thought we would go and be gigolos and try our chances and get work as actors on films in Rome. There was word on the grapevine that there was work for people of colour there. I did not like the scene there at all, but I got a job in theatre pulling the curtains. They did a production of a play called *Shakespeare in Harlem*, which was by Langston Hughes, one of the pioneering black writers of the Harlem Renaissance. Hughes turned up there. I watched that happening and I thought, 'I can do this!' So I decided to come back to London where I started writing about West Indians in London and Trinidad. A friend of Horace's, Rowland Reece, at the ICA [the Institute of Contemporary Arts], was looking for plays on black issues. This was when the ICA was still a wild place and things were happening.

Places like the Royal Court put on my plays. I was in the right place at a time when people were looking for my kind of plays and I was doing them. People were open to new things at the time and there weren't that many plays about West Indians in London. The key for me was that I used the natural dialect.

It was a particular person at the Royal Court who had the enlightenment and wanted to look at other people's culture. His name was Norman Beaton and also a guy named Ed Berman. They first ran the Green Banana Theatre. There was a black culture thing that was going on at the time. It transmogrified into the theatre that put on the plays at the ICA. It was a lively joint. Norman was running it so it had to be a swinging joint.

There was the hippy thing going on, people were just kind of grooving. It was a nice time and nice atmosphere. It's funny because people kind of dispersed into camps, some went on the hippy trail and some went on the political trail. The whole Black Power movement from America was really happening. Darcus Howe, Michael de Freitas, Stokely Carmichael and Dick Gregory were organising protests and rallies.

The brotherhood has definitely faded out since, the sense of togetherness. I will always have the spirit of the '60s. That sense of togetherness, it was real. It's been diluted because of the native culture of oppression.

A lot of our West Indians moved to this neighbourhood where I live, Queen's Park, because it was cheap and the railways nearby could get them to work. They came in to all the surrounding neighbourhoods around here and bought the run-down houses and now they are worth millions.

→ Mustapha at his home in Queen's Park, 2013.

The Asians too give a lot of black kids experience and jobs in computers, technology and business. It makes sense. You hire a black guy 'cause black people seeing a black guy will go in there. They don't have all these colonial hang-ups. It's business.

Economically some have done well and their children have too. Which would now be the black middle classes, the guys in the City and all that. You would have never dreamed about that, not long ago. The leaps that have been made!

The Asian sense of family is something that the West Indians have forgotten about because of the colonial influence. All they know is England. It's a big problem. They know what they are supposed to be, but they don't know what they are and this leads to a lot of grief.

I used to think theatre could be used for social change, but now I don't know. Although you throw a pebble in a stream and a ripple starts, you don't know where it's going.

In terms of my writing, I wanted to address and influence a black audience to learn about their culture and their roots. I coded it in such a way but this was the message. You could see the change and how the consciousness was being spread from one to another. In response to this I wrote a play called *Black Pieces* about the politicising and how it was being spread, passed like a rugby ball from one to another.

I can only speak for London but there is more mingling and contact from people from different cultures than anywhere else in the world.

Communities Lost and Found 135

VAL MILNER-BROWN
WRITER AND ENVIRONMENTAL ACTIVIST

I never went back to Ghana where I was born but when I look back I am happy with the real life I lived over here; well, … nearly all of it.

I first came to England in the mid-1960s. It was strange but interesting growing up in London and being an outsider on the inside of the 1960s. Never belonging and yet part of the inspiration or zeitgeist which formed the decade of revolution.

I was born in Kumasi, Ghana, but in those days it was called the Gold Coast. My two sisters and my brother didn't really belong there either because my father was a foreigner, a Jamaican who had come to Africa seeking adventure. My father had received a classic British education in a public school in Jamaica. He was virtually the only black kid and when he had children, his sole ambition was to give them the best education and without him ever having visited the motherland himself, he packed his kids off alone to the great colonial seat. He never knew that he had sent us to a slum in Ladbroke Grove! He, like many others, thought that England was Bertie Wooster, Jane Austen, Noël Coward, Graham Greene – that class.

At 14, I was taken by an English boyfriend to my first hippy pad and it was the real psychedelic experience: lava lamps mystically swirling colours on the walls, people sitting around doing nothing, in a state of purity and in touch with their highest selves. They called each other 'cats' and 'chicks' and instead of leaving a place or a country, they 'split' – a verb suggesting so much energy suddenly in the changing of location, so detached from anything, anywhere, anyone. And that is how my generation seemed to me. You just couldn't count on anyone to be hanging around if the 'vibe' wasn't right. As for me, I was quickly accepted into the 'scene', with my lanky self, soft voice and big gooey eyes and talk of beauty and loving clouds. Overnight I went from being called a 'jungle bunny' to being the real deal.

Everyone thought I was super cool, the token black. At this stage I looked like a female Jimi Hendrix, big afro, tight flared velvets, bandana, able to strum a few basic chords and sing a song or two in the dead of night with everyone sitting cross-legged profoundly searching for enlightenment. And there I was in their midst; in their eyes, the pure, unspoiled African, a Caliban or Robinson Crusoe, a mystical figure. I never belonged.

I am the sum total of all the parts of my life, sad, ironic, lonely, misplaced, out of time and in the time. Having grandchildren finally placed my feet solidly on England's green and pleasant land. The children are totally British but I try to instil in them some connection with where their grandma originally came from and to reap the reward from having this other cultural experience flowing somewhere in their blood and psyche.

← Val outside her old house in Bassett Road, Ladbroke Grove.

I know that in my small way, I was part of a changing society. Those middle-class hippies found comfort and inspiration in me because, although I was silently crying inside, I was not in any way shaped by the constraints of middle-class England.

↓ Schoolgirl Valerie aged 11.

↓ Her sister Lou's wedding day in London. From left to right: brother-in-law Mick, Lou, Val, Mae, a friend and Dick Nuttall.

↓ Val and her sister Lou on a camping trip with the soon-to-be father of her children, Dick Nuttall.

→ Val on Bassett Road in the 1960s hanging out and watching the world go by with her friend Cynthia.

↓ With the first of her four daughters in Waterlow Park, North London, 1974.

Wolverhampton disco, 1978.

CHAPTER SIX

WEEKENDS

For recreation, we would do blue-spot gram parties, you know, make a party at each other's home on a Saturday night. Bring ginger wine, curried goat, salt mackerel and green banana. You would soak the fish, then boil it and then fry up some onion and ting, put together.

DOROTHY YOUNG

CHAPTER SIX

WEEKENDS

THE LIGHTER SIDE OF LIFE

People often cling to entertainment as a means of psychological survival. In the midst of an alien, often difficult and lonely world, socialising with fellow countrymen is invariably an opportunity for any migrant to tune into their roots, meet potential life partners and forget about the hardships they might be experiencing.

As there are infinite stars in the sky, so there are infinite experiences of the same situation. However, the people we spoke to shared common threads and we can lift from their tales what it was like for them to settle in and enjoy life through socialising and entertainment. The common theme was the need for the warm feeling of belonging to a group or the familiar faces on your Saturday night clubbing route, the Sunday service at church, the banter with the market traders or a neighbour's friendly smile when you feel alone. That said, there were interesting differences in the way entertainment and social life was experienced by early migrant Indians and by Afro-Caribbeans.

For Afro-Caribbeans, the blues dance was a central part of their social lives, often clannish in that it would be a legacy passed down through the family. The home sound system, called the blue-spot gram, was also an excuse to congregate with neighbours and family. Every Caribbean-populated street would have one of these state-of-the-art furniture consoles that featured a turntable with storage for a bar.

A new release, imported hot off the press from the famous Studio One label in Jamaica, was always a good reason to get a blues party going.

Gathering together, in the drab and oppressive surroundings in which they were trying to gain a foothold, would be spiritually uplifting to Caribbeans. The lyrics would air relevant issues for the black community and diaspora: constraint, liberty, and punishment from the law. A forum to make sense of their world.

West End nightclubs were harder to access so black people's nightlife was driven underground. Shebeens were unlicensed places where you could buy alcohol and stand up next to a sound system for the night in the pitch-black, womb-like sanctity of the room. They were spartan in their distillation of elements: a DJ and speakers, a place where black people could create a contemplative space, their own cultural bubble of shared understanding.

Beyond this, there were live centres of clubbing in central London, Manchester and Birmingham, led by the Caribbean musicians and later by DJs. The latest tunes, the latest dance craze and of course fashion were all driven by the Caribbean influence.

The mingling of youths from all races dancing to the same beat was not just a flirtation or British kids' desire for connoisseurship of an alien culture but a real, shared experience and an escape from the sullen atmosphere of post-war Britain. Club culture was a middle ground, a bonding experience in itself.

For the Indian community, things were, at least initially, more sombre. Many of the first newcomers were men who had travelled alone to carve out a life before sending for their families. Men would gather at the library to catch up on the news back home, reading the local gazettes. Regular Saturday afternoon trips to the Asian cinema were also a huge highlight. Later on,

A new release, imported hot off the press from the famous Studio One label in Jamaica, was always a good reason to get a blues party going.

← Asian teenagers outside a cinema, 1980.

Jazz dancing in the dance halls where black men held dominion.

Indian films shown at places like the Ilford Odeon would be an appropriate form of leisure. They were a far cry from the restraint of a British audience at the cinema : here one would strain to hear the film over the babble and calling out from the Indian audience.

People would come from miles around to see the films and would travel by bus at midnight when it was finished. There were Indian general managers who realised there was a need for this.

For the Indian and Afro-Caribbean communities, both then and now, places of worship were fundamental to their recreational experience as it was not only a chance to worship but also an important form of social connection. However, in those days it was not always easy to join an English church, as the initial response from the congregation could be frosty and suspicious. Home-worship groups were therefore formed in people's living rooms until they were later able to edge their way into public buildings of worship. The musical forms of spiritual worship were quite different to those of the white population.

Rather than pipe organs or pianos, the Indians brought instruments like the sitar and bhangra drums. The Afro-Caribbean communal gatherings of dance and worship were distinctive for their participative 'call and response' form during worship.

Today, both Indian and Caribbean faces can be seen across the entertainment industry – in music, sport, theatre, film and television. They brought the DJ culture to the entertainment industry in the UK. Yoga and meditation are a valued part of the culture here and within Christian church life – alternative forms of worship, arguably more fluid and vibrant than the typically understated British style.

Club culture was a middle ground, a bonding experience in itself.

I was a college headmaster in India and most of my Indian friends here at the time were also well educated. After a long week of work, we would enjoy relaxing in the park or in the library at the weekend, catching up on current affairs in all the international and UK news bulletins.

PIARA SINGH BAINS

In those days, I would go to the blues dance till 4am, then go home, get changed and go on duty. They were good days but you can't do it now! I would work a 48-hour shift but I'd take Saturday off to get my hair done, get a dress and off to dance, you know. We were happy. DOROTHY YOUNG

↓ Indian men in the park playing cards.

→ Dorothy Young and friends on a night out.

→ A trip to Kew with the church group. A good excuse to get dressed up.

Weekends 145

We had no real community but went on trips to the seaside on a coach organised by our music group. We would go out dressed to the hilt. The funny thing was, no one would ever set foot in the water! We would load up our coach with rice and peas and whatnot and go to the beach.

MAE MILNER-BROWN

↑ Teenagers day-trip to the seaside, Skegness, 1972

→ The seafront, Bognor Regis, 1967.

RALPH ADU
MUSICIAN/WORDSMITH

Even in today's eclectic Brixton, Adu must elicit stares as he saunters the streets in his uniform of leather trousers, neat long dreadlocks ornamented with silver pieces, dark glasses and a gap-toothed grin. Adu looks the true rocker he is but with a twist; a wide Kente cloth is swept across his shoulders and a regal cane in hand – a symbol of his prestigious lineage; his ancestral home of the Ashanti kingdom, Ghana. This African prince feels that London has been a good host to him. In the 1960s Adu flew to England to be taken under the wing of his uncle. However, after hanging out for a while in London with musicians and arty types, and recording a single 'Bye Bye Now My Rose' (released by President Records) Adu decamped to Germany. He followed a bohemian lifestyle drenched in blues and rock 'n' roll music – a career spanning nearly four decades. Caught up in London life, Adu has not been back to Ghana since. Adu is so passionate about London he was in no doubt as to where he wanted to be photographed – outside his favourite haunt, the famous blues establishment the 12 Bar Club on Denmark Street. Famous acts that played at the club in their early days include Martha Wainwright, Joanna Newsom, KT Tunstall (all of whose first London dates were at the 12 Bar), Damien Rice, Keane, The Libertines and Regina Spektor. The club's building was originally constructed as a stable. It was renamed as the 12 Bar Club in 1994 and enjoyed huge success before its closure in 2015. He speaks about this place and how it felt full of possibilities. He also talks about the Foundry poetry club in Shoreditch, which unearthed poets such as Vic Lambrusco, Pete Doherty (of the Libertines), Elena Bond, the late Simon Monkhouse, but also remembers the threat of the National Front in nearby Hoxton, which he says is now 'cleaned up and beautiful, full of restaurants and clubs'. The struggle of life is lived day by day rather than analysed and it is only by talking about the past that he gains a perspective.

London is crowded now. It's better. Gastronomy is good. There has never been any 'good old days' as far as I have known. I tour and I still think that London is the best city in the world.

Ralph revisiting his old haunt the 12 Bar Club where 'the greats' have played – including himself!

One word to describe London when he first arrived? 'Weird'. One word to describe your London now? 'Fantastic'.

Sheron at her seventh birthday party.

Being Jamaican is cool, from our athletes to our entertainers. Everyone wants to be able to say Irie Mon!

SHERON PEARSON
DJ HOST ON *THE CONDUIT SHOW*

My grandparents loved music, especially my grandmother, but you'd better not be playing any reggae music on Sunday. It was strictly Jim Reeves or gospel music then. Her favourite song was 'I Remember' by Laurel Aitken and my granddad's favourite was 'Ten Commandments' by Prince Buster. They used to 'trace' one another with music. It was hilarious. I guess they never realised that they were the frontrunners of today's sound clash.

They had a blue-spot gram. One side had the 45s, 38s and LP records and another section had the drinks. The knick-knacks stood proudly atop the gram resting on a highly starched doily.

As I got older, my love of music was nurtured by my father who was a long-time soundman. His friends were all soundmen. I'm talking about Count Suckle, Sofrano B, Duke Vin, V-Rocket. I became steeped in music. My dad actually took me to a blues night where he was playing. That's where I met my first serious boyfriend. Mum certainly wasn't pleased when she found out about it and that put the mockers on further excursions with Dad.

Growing up in South London, I remember many memorable party sessions. Railton Road in its demolition stage after the Brixton riots provided the perfect hidey-hole for the transient blues parties that were held every night of the week. Thick black garbage bags blocked out the windows so you never knew what time it was.

We'd stumble out at the end of the sessions, blinking like frightened owls at the high midday sun. As one site shut down, two or three sprung up as replacements. The blues provided income for 'sufferers' and entrepreneurs alike. You could buy single cigarettes or champagne, depending on your pocket and taste.

But most of all, the thing that tied us all together was the love of the music and the chance to hear some good, good reggae and soul. Those truly were the days of our lives.

The music of those times took its lead from Jamaica for the main, but later the youths in England created their own sound. This was the birth of lovers rock, not to be confused with anything that Dennis Brown, Gregory Isaacs or Beres Hammond performed.

The lovers rock sound was the expression of British youth and their answer to what was coming out of Jamaica and also a reflection of their lives as second-generation immigrants.

There are too many names to mention for fear of missing out some of the key players in the British lovers rock genre, so I'll just give a tribute to two of the main proponents who are no longer with us: Jean Adebambo and Bevan 'Bagga' Fagan from the group Matumbi.

My stepfather was a soundman and my mother was a raver, she still is actually. My grandparents had a blues party for me every year for my birthday, until one of my uncles was murdered and another seriously injured. I attended my first blues dance with my stepfather at the age of 14 and met the love of my life. When my stepfather found out, he swore never to take me to another dance. I knew soundmen like Coxsone, Sofrano B, Neville King and many others. The sound system was a way for those who had migrated to England to keep in touch with their culture and the music from their native Jamaica.

Everywhere you look and in every stratum of life in England, you can see the influence of the Caribbean. It has had a seismic influence on fashion and music. There's the biggest street festival, started in London, the Notting Hill Carnival. Fashion is inspired by African and Caribbean culture and colours.

Liberty Cinema in Southall, 1977.

SATISH AND MAYA SEHGAL
CONVENIENCE STORE OWNERS

We came in 1972 after my dad had come previously, brought into the rag trade here by a friend.

I was hoping to stay for a while and go back home as I missed the lifestyle in Uganda. Then the coup happened with Idi Amin and I have stayed ever since.

It was a very lonely existence; we had to get used to the English dialect and ways. We have learnt so much from Mother England and can now have a good rapport with the English. I can speak to West Indians in their dialect for a laugh with them too! It was more difficult with the Indians as they can be quite snobbish. They think if they have been here a year longer they are better than us.

We didn't have temples of worship in the beginning. We would have a little shrine at home and worship there. Then we had the Hare Krishna temple in Watford. George Harrison from the Beatles donated the estate.

Not many places to socialise really, except going to the cinema. For entertainment, we would get together at the weekend. At the cinema nearby there were Indian general managers who realised there was a need for showing Asian cinema.

It was a routine every Friday or Saturday night that we would go in the minibus to the Odeon in Ilford or Mile End and watch Hindi films. It was our only social time really. During the films, people would shout out all kinds of things. Indians are very noisy. They can't keep quiet. People would come from miles around to see the films and we would travel by bus at midnight when it was finished.

Indian cinema was an appropriate setting for youngsters to mingle and for family gatherings. The IWA-owned Dominion Cinema, which showed Bollywood films, was a mainstay of the British Asian community in its heyday, attracting leading actors from India and more than 8,000 cinemagoers each week. There were also packed houses for its boxing, wrestling and cultural nights.

We always had the weddings too, although they have changed. When we were married we had over a thousand people at our wedding, whereas our daughter only wants 200. Just the close friends and family she knows. When we go to weddings now, I see lots of inter-racial marriages – it's becoming quite common. My niece and my son have children with West Indian partners. We decided early on we either go back or we adopt the way of life here and let our children lead. Our family always did give us a little leeway and we won't fight over religion.

'GUS' OSMOND PHILIP
RETIRED BT ENGINEER

We used to go to a blues dance they used to call it – just a table for a bar and a sound system. They came about in this way because they couldn't get premises. In the '80s people ran what they used to call shebeens. First it was Saturdays then it was Fridays and Saturdays. The name comes from New Orleans blues music. The first reggae tunes were based on New Orleans music they call the blues. You'd go to the record shop and you would say, 'I'm going to buy two blues tunes.'

Blues – that's the music they played in the sound systems so even when the sound became reggae the name just stayed. Wherever there was a West Indian community there was always blues.

I heard about blues nights from leaflets guys would give out outside the record shops; this is where young black guys used to gather on a Friday or Saturday afternoon. They would have sound system competitions. Immigration was still going on and young guys fresh from Jamaica would have the latest crazes.

The police would shut the shebeens down. It wasn't a licensed place. Although they liked it because they would let the thing run for four nights and then come in and take what they wanted like the drugs. Sometimes when they left after a raid, it would start up again.

A lot of musicians would come there, like the Rolling Stones. The Mangrove was first a gambling joint, and then a herb joint, so the police closed it down. It was a place where people would sit and talk and exchange views. It was a place where active resistance against the police could happen.

Eventually people had had enough. The youths have moved up a level in terms of what they expect. The way you would dance, propped up against a sweaty wall all night; sometimes we came back from a dance with wallpaper stuck on our backs from the wall! Anyway, this type of music is not played any more. Young people have a lot more variety these days.

We call it the front line: it is All Saints Road. The Mangrove restaurant was run by a so-called community leader Frank Critchlow. It was a black, upbeat kind of place. It was a 24-hour market there. He lost his right to run it in 1969. You would hear how he was a community leader and so on. However, I cannot see what positive he brought to the youths except teach you how to break into a car and sell stuff on the front line. He used to get us to rally against the police, against police brutality and so on. Those guys, the pop stars, associating themselves with that place would make it look not so threatening to the rest of the world. Any way to ease off the tension helped. It was all about the exposure you know. On TV, they made an effort to bring things together. They would talk positive about black artists and cover songs by black artists. A lot of black people at last had a feeling that others were all going through the same thing as you.

English people heard reggae music before the rest of the world because it was all over here. It was how West Indian people lived. It exploded and became part of the landscape. It was something we could fall back on and call ours. There were no radio stations for us; eventually we would get an hour or two on Saturday.

I heard about blues nights from leaflets guys would give out outside the record shops; this is where young black guys used to gather on a Friday or Saturday afternoon. They would have sound system competitions. Immigration was still going on and young guys fresh from Jamaica would have the latest crazes.

← Gus on the guitar in his living room.

↑ Gus with dreads.

← Reminiscing on all that has gone on down the All Saints Road.

← The now closed Sarm West (formerly Island) recording studio, which played a part in creating the black music culture in Ladbroke Grove. Local talent and international music artists would come to record here.

→ Gus and friends outside the Tabernacle, Ladbroke Grove. This community centre has served the diverse community as a youth centre, arts and music hub and a local and topically themed Christmas pantomime.

↓ Gus on his steel drum.

In the '70s the pirates (radio) came. It made them realise there was another set of people to recognise in the community. Even the white kids liked the reggae; it became commercial very soon with bands like UB40 and Madness.

Weekends

The establishment BBC broadcasters did not have the finger on the pulse, they weren't connected to this world and were slow on the uptake, not fully realising the potential of this cultural explosion.

FAZE 1 FM 90.9

	MON	TUE	WED	THUR	FRI	SAT	SUN
7-9 AM	PAUL RICHARDS			HENRY VIII			S.J.B.
9-12 AM	BOOKER.T					DOUBLE M	GROOVE RIDER
12-2 PM	D.J. FABIO				DESI.9 + BARRY WHITE	L.S.B	
2-4 PM	ANDREW DAZZLER	COMMAND B	HEAVY DUTY	MENDOZA	CLAZZY J	WOOD HOUSE	SPUNKY G
4-6 PM	HEAVY DUTY	FUNK E.D.	CLAZZY J	FUNK E.D.		COMMAND B	CLAZZY J
6-8 PM	L.S.B		D.J Y	JAM MASTER C	D.J. JAYNE		
8-10 PM	CRIME MASTER T	SPUNKY G	ANDREW DAZZLER	COMMAND B	G.I JOE	JAM MASTER C	MENDOZA
10-1 PM-AM	CLIVE RARE GROOVE B.	CRIME MASTER T	JAM MASTER C	PAUL RICHARDS	D.J Y	CLAZZY J	DESI.9 + BARRY WHITE
1-3 AM	GROOVE RIDER	DESI.9 + BARRY WHITE	S.J.B	CLIVE RARE GROOVE B	ESTER J	TIL DJ L.A	4 VICKY P
3-5 AM	COMMAND B	ANDREW DAZZLER	COMMAND B	ANDREW DAZZLER	D.J DEAN	D.J DEAN	ISSAC J
5-7 AM	VICKY P						

Mailing Address: 5 Oval Place, London SW8
Studio No: 0860 378938   Page No: 01-367 6767   Unit 2255

'Oh my gosh! The music just turns me on!'

The influence of pirate radio on popular culture should not be underestimated. While Radio Caroline is famous as one of the earliest and most influential of the pirates, black pirate stations contributed greatly to the phenomenon and through it influenced a myriad of trends in music.

The name 'pirate' came from the ships where such stations could broadcast beyond the reach of the law. However, the black stations were set up in any place they could: the back of a TV repair shop, hidden at the side of a greengrocers, or on the roof of a high-rise block of flats. All you needed was an antenna and someone who could fix you up with a makeshift transmitter. But they were often within the reach of the law.

They would be raided by the police regularly. Singer Sylvia Tella remembers the arrests made on these dens: 'They were getting arrested every week!'. But they were born out of necessity as the mainstream stations would only offer a little time to the genres favoured by black people.

The groundswell in the pirates' popularity spread across the nation – it spoke directly to people, giving them the sounds they craved and informing them of club-night happenings and new trends.

Initially it was a way for black people to find a connection in an estranged world but it was also a portal and gateway for understanding and connecting to black culture for all.

The vernacular and the music styles of these vibrant channels were supported by specialised record shops like Hawkeye and Black Market Records. Intertwined with the clubbing scene this all became a lively underground world. Eventually the major record labels picked up on this storm created by black Britons. In recognition of the popularity of black music and the business opportunities that it provided, the government finally gave way and issued the first licence to the pirate station Kiss FM in 1989. The black music that was broken through these channels, such as reggae and dancehall, profoundly influenced the wider music scene.

White English DJs like Tony Blackburn and Tim Westwood were the acceptable face for black music during the 1970s and 80s. More recently black representatives like Twin B (head of A&R at Atlantic Records) have become celebrity DJs and the commercial face of popular radio.

However, mainstream radio still can't keep up with the agility and creativity of black and Asian young people who are now using the internet to break new ground and stream relevant content, not just for their communities but for young people from all backgrounds.

← Faze 1 FM Radio schedule.   ↑ Gus's momento wall.

Notting Hill Carnival, 1981.

CHAPTER SEVEN

BREAKING BARRIERS

*Put my ear to the ground,
listen to the people.*

PETER MINSHALL,
CO-FOUNDER OF THE FIRST
NOTTING HILL CARNIVAL

A demonstration organised by the Asian community in protest against racist immigration laws and deportation, 1978.

CHAPTER SEVEN

BREAKING BARRIERS

GOING BEYOND OUR STATION

In the 1960s and 70s there were so many walks of life where black people and Asians just weren't expected to feature.

Home Office correspondence has revealed that the British had very stereotypical expectations of immigrants. They wanted Commonwealth subjects to remain in subservient, background jobs like manual labour and cleaning within their new British home. Indeed, migrants were invariably recruited into low-level jobs and overlooked for promotions. They found that doors that were open to the British were shut to them. Some early migrants did manage to make progress to middle-rung roles, for instance from station porter to manager or hospital domestic to nursing staff. However, more frequently we heard sentiments such as 'they had quotas on management roles reserved for the English people' and 'it was impossible for black people to gain pupillage'.

There is also evidence in the Home Office correspondence at the time of the fear surrounding migrants and the threat they were perceived to pose to British society. It is perhaps unsurprising, therefore, that many who broke with the stereotypical mould often faced resistance and negativity from the British.

Migrants consequently felt that they had to work twice as hard and be twice as good as British people to make any progress in life. The early pioneers broke down a multitude of significant barriers they were faced with and, in doing so, paved the way for new generations to follow.

A myriad of new initiatives set up by migrants were forged out of hardship and discrimination. Today, we can see the legacy of these gritty, quietly determined men and women in a plethora of ways across the country. Breakthroughs in commerce were achieved

I was aware that the black community always seemed to be on the other side of the docks. I just thought the law was not on our side and the only way to change that was to get involved. I just felt that it was a way to achieve some justice. I might have broken some barriers but it hasn't been easy. You do attract enemies, but I tend not to complain about those. Glass half full!

LORD TAYLOR OF WARWICK

most notably by the Indians and breakthroughs for West Indians occurred mostly in sports, media and the entertainment world. With entrepreneurial spirit and steely persistence, the many Indian and Bengali families who set up their own restaurants have been pivotal in enabling curry to be affectionately adopted as the national dish. Indeed, virtually every high street in the country has its own curry house these days.

Perhaps most importantly, today there is more diversity of talent in different walks of life. Whether the changes have been big or small, the first-generation migrants had to fight hard to break down the barriers they faced. While the battle is far from over, the people who began the effort had to fight hardest, and need to be honoured for their persistence, personal grit and, at times, outright bravery.

However, there are still barriers today which need to be broken and we are probably a long way from having a black prime minister in Britain. Black people and Asians are still significantly under-represented in the business arena and while there was a movement in the 1980s to bring greater diversity into media, by the late 1990s, there had been a big shift back to media being more dominated by white people. Barriers aren't always broken for good – they often re-emerge – so the battle has certainly not ended.

In the late 1970s the discussion taking place at the Carnival Arts Committee encouraged the political 'return to Africa' ideology. This was different to the Black Power movement and Pan Africanism that was pushed by the competing Carnival Development Committee (CDC). The CDC objectives were for the Carnival to be a strictly fun and inclusive affair. The West Indian community felt carnival was something they could call theirs and they felt proud to take over the streets of Notting Hill once a year. The majority of West Indians now saw themselves as an integral part of British society taking part in its institutions and benefiting from its social services, and they wanted to share their cultural celebration with the world. The symbolism of this union is shown in the masks themselves; British kings and queens and Robin Hood would appear next to African liberation fighters and other representatives from the Black Hall of Fame.

Carnival: a truly democratic expression where the body, desires and sensuality are a far cry from the imperialist and elitist art forms of Britain's past.

Carnival brings together people of all classes, ethnicities and religious groupings – a manifestation of what is so joyous and free about our multicultural heritage here in the UK.

With its origins in South America and Trinidad, carnival has always had the potential to foster friendship and integration as people enjoy a party and revelling together. It takes the edge off a potentially conflict-ridden nation and for at least a few days a year shows a glimpse of harmony. This vision metamorphosed into a new culture, a new population of Britons.

In the Notting Hill Carnival, reggae and calypso songs play out the expression of oppression the youths can feel and express bitter criticism of the police and endemic racism. And also of each other.

A meeting of the Notting Hill Carnival Development Committee, London, 19 January 1977. From left: secretary James Cumming, treasurer Russell Henderson, chairman Selwyn Baptiste, Zigi Constantine, George Binney, Robin Tuck and Lord Sam.

← Southall Town Hall, September 1974. Southall became a battleground for issues relating to race, immigration and social policy. There were small breakthroughs. Southall Committee protested about 'bussing' Indian children to special schools out of town so that they could learn together instead of holding back English-speaking children.

↓ Zadie Smith carried by her mother, Yvonne Bailey-Smith, at the Notting Hill Carnival.

Breaking Barriers

DHARAM DASS
BARRISTER AND POLITICAL RADICAL

There were really not many overseas students who came through the bar at that time. There was only one Chair from Uganda and the only person who was older than me was a Kenyan man who was a judge.

I found it impossible to get pupillage. I applied for every job. Eventually Greville Janner gave me the pupillage. He was a remarkable member of parliament. He used to take me home for Sunday dinners. He was very nice to me. But the clerk of the chambers would negotiate the fee between the solicitor and the barrister, then pass on the briefs to whomever he liked in the chambers. I was a junior going in and out of court. Socially, I was really distant. But the clerk of the chambers had no knowledge of who the Indians were so he never passed anything to me independently. All the solicitors I knew said they would like to send me a brief; they would send the briefing but the clerks would not pass them on to me.

I only voiced these thoughts after I went to Berkeley in North America. I came back to the UK for two years then I started writing a book on racism. In 1970, Enoch Powell said that all immigrants should be sent back to their country by giving them a £2,000 cheque. I was overseas when I heard his 'Rivers of Blood' speech and I took a plane straight to London, went to Wolverhampton and applied to be a candidate against him. I brought an American colleague back with me.

We formed a party called the Human Rights Coalition. We set up the office in Wolverhampton and began a campaign – not to be a member of parliament but to speak against an idiot. What did Powell expect all these chaps to think, especially the people from Punjab who sold their land and came and made their houses, their homes here, and were working here?

← Dharam Dass election poster when he ran against Enoch Powell.

The Labour Party was accusing me of dividing the immigrant vote. There were 4,000 Indians who were members of the local Labour Party in Wolverhampton. The existing Labour representative said they really need this vote so please withdraw your application this year and in the next election, we'll give you a safe seat. I said, 'I'm not here to be a member of parliament. I'm here to protest.' Anyhow, my conscience had told me I'd achieved what I needed to achieve.

I did meet Enoch Powell, but only after the elections. The day before the elections, we had radio and TV coverage. I asked, 'Am I going to live in this country under these conditions? No way. I am not living in this country myself, I'm going away from here.' However, I then set up my own business and made money.

My experience as a barrister has been very disappointing. I'm not going to be associated with anybody in the legal profession in this country. It's a racist approach.

RUSSELL HENDERSON MBE (1924–2015) MUSICIAN AND CO-FOUNDER OF THE NOTTING HILL CARNIVAL

I was born in Trinidad and I came to London in 1951. I was always a musician. I thought there was a void in piano tuning; the older ones were dying out. I went to the Northern Polytechnic in Holloway and within the first year people started to get news there was a West Indian pianist in town.

I did a lot of nightclub gigs. Then a job was offered to me to put a band together. I got a drummer from Trinidad and we formed a sort of trio and from there we were playing all the time, events happened and the Notting Hill Carnival came into play.

I was the only person with a steel band at the time. A social worker called Rhaune Laslett was putting on a street theatre with the kids off Ladbroke Grove. She asked me if I would bring my steel band and play a bit for the kids. We had the pans round our necks, the street was blocked off at both ends and I went to the chaps and said, 'Move your barriers. We're going to make a little block and come back.' They had a clown doing a little juggling and a donkey ride.

By the time we got out there, people started following this novelty and the rounds got bigger and bigger. We went all around Queensway and back. So, the next year Laslett thought it was so fantastic we could do it again. There were no costumes involved at this time so she started to get the neighbourhood involved. Within three years we had committees. That's the start of the Notting Hill Carnival – spontaneous!

An important point is that this was in April. It was so cold then, so it was moved to the summer. We didn't encounter any resistance to the Carnival at the beginning. When we did the parade, people just crowded around to see this colourful show.

I'm not sure how I feel about the Carnival now. Some changes are good and some bad. I am not happy about them changing the route, as they are not familiar with the neighbourhood. They're also bringing a lot of policemen on the day of the Carnival and I'm not too happy with the stewarding.

Carnival is a spontaneous thing. It is organised to fall on a public holiday so that communities can come together. I call it another Lord Mayor Show now. You form a band and it is all regimented. So you can't get into that part of it, the real carnival. Of course, it is bigger now so you need a bit of control but not in a way to kill the passion! You have to look at security all round the world. These aspects have affected spontaneity all over the world.

I never imagined we would make such an impact on London. I was just doing a little job. The band I started was called Band Nectar and I still play every year at Carnival. If you take part in a band you get a different perspective.

There's been a big change in how West Indians are in London compared to when I first came in 1951. West Indians would talk to each other and end up in the same neighbourhoods such as Brixton and Ladbroke Grove. Every street in the West End had piano bars and most pubs had a piano so there was a lot of work.

As a minority, of course you have your prejudices all the way, some very subtle and some downright insulting like, 'You black so-and-so.' Those who didn't experience that kind of thing were lucky. On the other side of it I got a lot of work on the back of my talent and exoticism. The insults did trouble me to a point. It's sad to see it because we were coming from a country where everyone was so polite and then you come and see people here were worse than you. You can't worry if people like you or not but if it stops you from getting work, then that is a problem. That is how I live my life.

As a musician, you were a few stripes ahead of the bus drivers. We used to play for all the society balls in the aristocratic circles. We were the talk of the town.

We didn't encounter any resistance to the Carnival at the beginning. When we did the parade, people just crowded around to see this colourful show.

HORACE OVÉ CBE
FILMMAKER AND DIRECTOR

I was always interested in making films. Trinidad had about 300 cinemas going back since the 1940s. It's a multicultural society so you had French films and Spanish films. My family were into putting on plays so I grew up in that sort of world and liked it very much. I came to Britain to check out the colonial masters of the Caribbean and Trinidad, and also to study films.

I was lucky enough to get a job as an extra on the *Cleopatra* film in 1961 with Elizabeth Taylor. I started as a Roman because they needed a guy with a nice complexion, like he's been in the sun, but when they moved the filming to Rome I was made a slave. It was interesting to me because this was the surrealist, this was the 'real' cinema, which took me beyond Hollywood, which had a great influence on my life and influenced my work a great deal. I also worked as a runner on sets to see how it was done. Then I thought I better go to film school.

My social and political comments were all about real life. It was not only about the world you were living in but the world in your head, the world in your dreams, the world that you think of but you don't tell anybody. A lot of films I made had that angle, for instance *Pressure*, the first black feature film in this country.

When you look at *Pressure* you see those corresponding worlds. I also use my knowledge of travelling in India and Africa as inspiration.

Things have changed in the industry for budding black film directors since the 1960s, but it was never easy. I was lucky in the sense of how I was brought up. I had parents who told me from a very young age that I have a right to get out there and do my thing. I was able to push doors open. Sure, sometimes you push the door and meet a real arsehole and sometimes you push the door open and the person says, 'Come in. Let's do something.' I think there is a problem for black and Asian kids and I still think they have to go beyond that. If the door wasn't open, I got my work made independently. I got financing and help from people who were interested in me.

After a lifetime of questioning the colonial empire and its residual troubles, it was weird being awarded a CBE by the Queen of England.

I think they have given it to me for my work. I have done a lot of documentaries approaching real life, social and political issues and people and their problems. Most of my films are based on that. A lot of people who know me asked me why I was accepting the CBE. I say, 'Why not? I have worked hard and they are honouring me for the work I have done so I am very happy about it.'

After a lifetime of questioning the colonial empire and its residual troubles, it was weird being awarded a CBE by the Queen of England.

Poster for the film *Pressure*.

These days, I do try to get around lecturing and encouraging young filmmakers to spread the message by saying, 'Come on guys, don't let racism stop you. Get out there and don't give up.'

LOUIS MAHONEY
(1938–2020) POLITICAL ACTIVIST AND ACTOR

I came to London in the 1950s to study medicine. At that time, Patrice Lumumba ('Mumba') had been arrested in the Congo conflict.

The images on the news of Mumba shackled in the back of a police van were spread on the front pages of newspapers. I had a beard like Mumba, so the children the next day were chanting 'Mumba, Mumba, Mumba'. I laughed. I grew up with a strong sense of humour and I knew to respond to it in any negative way would cause more problems.

My impression before I came here was that the streets were paved with gold but teaching here really gave me insight into the other side of English life, that is the poverty, the uneducated, the tramps, so I never felt inferior in any way. Remember Philip Smith in the TV series *Rising Damp*? The son of an African chief, he didn't have the slightest feeling of inferiority. However, in terms of the buildings and infrastructure, sure, I was very impressed with it.

At that time, I stayed initially in Hans Crescent in Knightsbridge, a holding place for overseas people from ex-British colonies, so you met people from Ghana, Nigeria and Jamaica. It was a meeting point at weekends, a centre if you like, of intellectual discussions not only political but swapping notes of where you came from. This was a time when the ex-colonies were becoming independent countries so there was a lot to talk about. Some became people involved in the United Nations, international law and so on.

I gave up medicine and moved away from these academic circles. I was keen on becoming an actor because my dad was principal of a school and very strict. I remember the first time I really saw him enjoy himself was when he came to my school play *Androcles and the Lion*. I played the lion cub and I could see him laughing and I thought, 'My God, I am making him laugh.'

Whilst I taught I was part of an amateur theatre group linked to Stratford East (previously Theatre Royal) with a lady called Joan Littlewood. We would perform *commedia dell' arte* in Leyton Park and she suggested I apply for the Central School of Speech and Drama, which I got into but did not complete because I was offered a job as an understudy at the Duke of York's.

It was very exciting and there weren't in fact any problems being a black actor in the West End theatre. There were quite a few well-known black actors at the time, people like Earl Cameron and Johnny Secker. Black writers such as Wole Soyinka were also writing for the West End. However, many white people said that the plays that they were doing were middle-class plays and had no place for black faces.

Around that time, I joined a group at the Royal Court under George Devine. They were focused on talent, not colour. We had a group called Theatre Machine and we improvised shows in pubs. The thing about that, they gave opportunities to any actor who showed promise irrespective of their background. That activity led me to the actors' union, Equity, and changed what they called the Coloured Actors Committee to the Afro-Asian Committee. We had seminars where we invited heads of drama schools. The GLC and the National Council insisted there would be a limit on the intake. I ended up being part of the examining group that went around various schools in the UK and Scotland to look at the philosophy of the school in order to grant them governing support and also have the facility to allow the students to become Equity members when they qualified.

My biggest disappointment is that, unlike America, we have not in Britain nurtured talented black and Asian actors.

My political activism was triggered by what was happening at the drama school and my involvement with Equity. It made me become much more of an activist and I became part of a movement to refuse to sell British TV programmes to apartheid South Africa.

The interesting thing about this was there was a black South African troupe with a show called *EpiTombe* that of course we were happy to receive. Normally when a group are brought over from abroad they are given an accommodation allowance and I discovered they were sleeping on a bus during the tour. The management said, 'Oh, that's what these people are used to.' I changed all that and got them into decent flats. At the end of the tour they did not want to go back to South Africa so I managed to get them refugee status in the UK but I needed to get them some work. I had just formed the Black Theatre Workshop and I got them to do a show called *The Sounds of Soweto*.

Back then there were eight to ten black theatre groups. There was much more focus on the lack of opportunity for black and ethnic minority groups in the '70s and '80s. There is a broad brush now and the minister of the Arts Council is quoted as saying that he does not look at figures now that we are all so integrated. The resulting thing is there are only a few specialised theatre groups now.

The Caribbeans' only perceptions of Africans was the sort that came from brainwashing TV programmes and films like *Tarzan*, so it was interesting when the Windrush generation came along and got the menial jobs while the Africans had come to study. There was a real divide.

Africans have a social structure, some sort of tribe and so on. This gives the Africans a sense of confidence, which was often a point of jealousy for the Caribbeans. People have said to casting directors, 'Oh, Louis is so political', which was a way of killing my career. In fact it worked in my favour when we had to do films like *Cry Freedom*. Because I was involved in the anti-apartheid movement and I was quite forceful about it, I was offered a choice of three different roles. I don't think that standing up for what you perceive as equality and fair play is going to affect your career if you are serious about the work you do.

One of the things that drew me to the culture of England was the idea that the meeting place for most people was the pub. Even then you could see in the pubs there was a class system: here was the public bar and there was the lounge bar. The ordinary workers would be in the public bar and in the posh area were the estate agents and doctors. That showed me how that particular structure in this society was. I never had a problem with my status and my interest was that I could talk to people in the public bar and the lounge bar and I could find out a lot more about how things worked in England.

I once went to tea with an English friend when I was a

student. He came from Cambridge and I went to his parents for the weekend. They were educated, nice people and I remember asking to be excused to go to the lavatory. When I came back sooner than they expected I could see them looking at the lip of my cup to see if my colour dropped off. For me there was nothing wrong with that because they didn't understand. It taught me that in fact to predispose that people don't like you because of the colour of your skin can often be a negative approach. Talking to people and meeting them, that discourse can dispel any preconceived ideas they may have had.

My biggest disappointment is that, unlike America, we have not in Britain nurtured talented black and Asian actors.

Over the last 20 or 30 years that I have been actively involved with Equity and the business I have seen a lot of talent come through. Many have worked with the national companies, have been acclaimed by the *Evening Standard* and have won awards but they have never nurtured them on to the next stage. Whereas with the white actress or actor, once you get an award of some kind, everyone wants to use you. I think this is because there is a subliminal racism within the system.

I remember attacking the Head of Drama at the BBC at a seminar. I said, 'Listen, things like *Holby City* and *Casualty* are not representative. When I was a medical student in the 1960s there were consultants from Ghana and Nigeria, yet we cannot see a black guy who is a registrar or a consultant on the programme.' He said, 'Oh, we are thinking of one at the moment. We have a guy called Hugh Quarshie.' I said, 'Yes, he's damn good and he's been there now for almost eight years!' So, it works but they just don't perceive us, you have to tell them. Same with the new programme *The Streets* set in Liverpool. There has been a black population in Liverpool since the sixteenth century! So why are there not characters to represent this?

The South African Broadcasting Corporation wanted to buy British programmes and with me sitting there they said, 'We would very much like to buy British programmes but there must not be any blacks in them. If there are any blacks in them they have to be servants or gardeners like in our country.' So, Equity organised a referendum, Performers Against Racism. I campaigned and I had a lot of support from people like Glenda Jackson and Julie Christie. We managed to stop any TV programmes being sold to South Africa. There was also a ban on British plays being performed in South Africa.

Breaking Barriers

Queen Mother Moore, a civil rights activist, holding Ajah, the baby brother of Ekua McMorris who is bottom right. Behind are Ekua's mother and Ekua's brother Tekla. The boy to the left is Yousef.

CHAPTER EIGHT

PASSING THE BATON

Well, we are now talking about third- and fourth-generation black British people. They are more British than the British, so whether or not they are accepted, they are taking their place in the only mother country they know.

SHERON PEARSON
DJ HOST ON *THE CONDUIT SHOW*

CHAPTER EIGHT

PASSING THE BATON

IT'S YOUR TURN NOW

I have no regrets about coming to this country. My husband was a wonderful man and we worked hard, and it has been a success. Our children understand our Indian culture but they have adopted the British culture as well. I'm so proud of them and these are real blessings in life. We are very lucky. SWARN KIRPAL

Undoubtedly, a huge amount of self-sacrifice was necessary for these early immigrants, but there was also a sense of success from what they had done for their children. Some of their lives were so sad and full of hardship because they did everything for their children. In many cases, their children thrived and succeeded but in others, the baton wasn't passed.

We heard some elders saying that youngsters don't know how easy they've got it now because they were given so much help. Many were saddened that the next generation were not always making the most of the opportunities they had been given, as evidenced by issues like gun crime, poor performance at school or youngsters not making the effort to fit in to British society.

Our overall sense was that immigrants wanted their children to embrace their new British home without losing affection for and understanding of their original culture. Expectations, attitudes and values were inevitably passed on in a way that is likely to continue shaping their children's lives.

The media has played a role in society's perceptions of black and Asian people in both good and bad ways. There has been a push to include black and ethnic minorities in the media and advertising and especially across the BBC. But being a minority means you are often not so well known by the majority and any representations of criminal youth – as in the black youths' association with gun crime and cases like the Rotherham grooming gangs in the news – tar all who look like the accused with the same brush. In this growing climate of fear the instinct to lash out without considering the facts has led to an increase in public support for far-right views in this country.

In June 2018, the nation marked the 70th anniversary of the arrival of the HMT *Empire Windrush* at Tilbury Docks with a service in Westminster Abbey. This followed the Windrush scandal a few months earlier; we have heard the horrific stories of how the children of that generation have lost jobs and livelihoods, been denied health and medical services, and been consigned to detention centres to await deportation to the Caribbean.

The then prime minister, Theresa May, had used the popular resentment around immigration to extend a tougher regime towards recognising the status of Windrush-generation Britons. In the 1950s and 60s, this generation was often let into this country without thorough paperwork but now this was used against them. This betrayal shocked both them and the nation. It showed the short-lived loyalty to once-British subjects and the vulnerability of their identity. The British Empire had been defended by Asian, African and West Indian troops, among others, in both world wars. The process of decolonisation was sped up after that war effort and as an act of gratitude Commonwealth citizens were permitted by the 1948 British Nationality Act to come to the UK. On the day that the *Windrush* arrived, the London *Evening Standard* carried the headline 'Welcome Home'. And the Act allowed people to enter, work and settle with their families.

What kept many immigrants going through the tough early periods was the hopes they had for their children and a vision for their success. There are stories of migration in all families' histories; stories of falling in love, of adventure and always the very human act of imagination and seeding the hopes of those who follow.

'Gus' Osmond Philip and his son.

DELORIS SMITH
RETIRED NURSE, BEREAVEMENT COUNSELLOR AND MOTHER OF SINGER BEVERLEY KNIGHT

I knew Beverley could sing before she could talk. They always sang at church and were encouraged to sing. The first time Beverley sang on her own in public was in nursery. She stood on a chair with a caterpillar suit on and sang 'Peter the Reject Eater'. From that day on till Beverley left she was in every production, I mean everything.

I always assumed Beverley would be doing gospel. But then when she did her first pop album I was still a bit worried.

You see in the papers that celebrities are taking drugs, which was worrying and all that, but I am a praying woman. I would ask God to keep her safe. I think if you talk to your children, they do listen. We always had quite a good friendship with our children and that has lasted. When she is putting her tracks together, she has us in the back of her mind.

There are so many memorable moments for me in Beverley's career. Meeting Annie Lennox and Courtney Pine was great but still, Beverley collecting her MBE award from the Queen was absolutely fabulous. In Buckingham Palace she walked arm's length from me – that close. The Queen gave out 90 MBEs in an hour. It was Beverley, Eddie, Beverley's manager Alan Edwards and me. We were briefed how to greet the Queen and all the footmen were ever so pleasant. We went to The Ivy restaurant afterwards and saw Roger Moore and other celebrities eating at other tables. It's not something you can really visualise ahead.

Beverley also decided to set up her own make-up line for black skins. Until MAC came along there wasn't much for black skins anyway. You would see the powder before you see them.

I used to think if I am going to look like that, forget it. Sheer frustration for Beverley drove her to create her own line. Iman brought out a line that we all started to use and actually that is what got me into experimenting with make-up finally.

The high fashion and beauty industry is very blatant about not giving black women a look-in. I was with my friend, looking at all the magazines in WHSmith: *Red*, *The Lady*, *Woman's Own* and *OK!* to name a few. There was nothing there aimed at the black community apart from *Black Hair* magazine so I said to my friend, 'Don't they think black people wear clothes? Don't they think we shop or do anything?' There is nothing in the world of beauty representing multicultural Britain. Yes, we have come a long way in the media especially, but there is a long way to go.

Some people say, 'Oh, I am so proud of you.' I watch Beverley all the time and bring all the cuttings and that, but you got some who don't say anything at all, yet of course they always want her to come to sing at the church and give autographs. People say, 'Oh, when are you moving house?' They assume you would move to a grander house and live a different lifestyle. I was shopping at my local supermarket and bumped into a local lady and she said, 'What are you doing shopping here? You got a famous daughter!' I said, 'This is my money and I am spending it wisely, thank you very much!'

In this house my children were taught that all men are equal. All people were created by God from the same mould. Why God decided to give us different orientation on the outside I don't know, but we are all the same.

Not in a million years would I have thought I would meet the Queen. I just can't believe this happened, especially this being the 'mother country' and Buckingham Palace.

My children were taught to be proud of who they are. If you respect yourself, others will respect you. Eddie always said, 'Nobody owes you anything, go out there and work hard.'

When we first came to England, my father worked in a steel factory called Baileys and Jones; a steel foundry. He worked with heat and he didn't like it. People came here because you were told it is the 'Mother Country'. You were told here you would have a better life. You work and work but it is not the kind of work you would do given the choice, you know. My dad was earning far less when he came to work in the foundry than when he was in Jamaica.

I came in November and a friend who had just started training as a midwife said I could get into specialist nursing with the training. I was not quite 17 but the matron let me start the training early. You had to live in the nurse's home in the hospital, which was lovely. I was able to have my own room. There were Trinidadians, Jamaicans and the rest were English girls. We were all in classes together doing our training; it was nice.

I had one Jamaican girl I was friendly with but I also became friends with a couple of English girls and even now, 40 years later, we are still friends. There are some people you just seem to click with.

I never have a chip on my shoulder, but the older girls would tell me it's because I was black. They had been training there longer and probably went to parties and mixed more. Some had been to the white church and weren't welcome, some of them had had that kind of experience. I had a very sheltered life with the church.

To be honest, sometimes I think it is the wrong attitude that attracts racism. I think people can have a chip on their shoulder and make excuses. Sometimes it's your own attitude that generates other peoples' attitude. I've always said I love my colour.

When I first moved to this street, we had some lovely neighbours. There was an old lady who lived on her own, she used to play bridge. My husband would drop her off but she would come back so late and wake us up shouting, 'Mr Smith, can you come and undo my zip?'

Involvement in the church has had an influence on the community around me. I think the predominantly black churches have now integrated. People are suspicious of others but when they go to your weddings or funerals you think, 'Hang on a minute, this is not what I thought of these people.' Mixed marriages and things like that have helped change things.

I think the impact of the church on the community has been good because it breaks down barriers. The church is open to everybody.

My work colleagues were watching *Songs of Praise* and they mentioned that if the churches were fun like this they would go. When they go to our church with the clapping and the singing and the joy, they enjoy it because they don't find it boring.

JENNI FRANCIS
ART EXPERT AND INTERNATIONAL MUSEUM PROFESSIONAL

Just under 20 years ago I took the decision to work for the Royal Academy of Arts because I wanted to work for the big institutions to make change. As Head of Press and Marketing, I worked on diverse and relevant exhibitions such as Anish Kapoor and David Hockney. I am proud of my record introducing the popular annual BBC summer television programme to the institution via internal advocacy and to a worldwide audience through collaboration with a small team on the inside. It is exciting as we have developed new audiences and increased sales.

At school I was a rebel and leader. However, I remember the school's careers advice – I was told I could be a telephonist at the General Post Office plugging wires in and out. Very few people felt they had the right to go to university and at school I was never told. We had a lot of freedom which was good in a way for our development but a shame as at school we were allowed to run amok and allowed to do our thing. I think we were the Lost Generation. I also think we were a generation where mental health issues started to come up. Contributing to that were the sus laws, and putting young men into prison. I remember feeling singled out when I submitted a good piece of work, being questioned if it was actually my work. I had three poems published. The teachers submitted it so I was proud of that.

Me and my eldest sister were among the first group of children to West Indian parents at the school. We went to a very mixed comprehensive school. But back then it was, do you like this person, do they like you regardless of colour? It's only when you go up the ladder you start to feel the divisions.

Because I had my boys young and I had something to prove, it was an extra driver for me to rise up as a strong woman. I came from a generation where we looked after our men. Our fathers and brothers would have dinner ready for them when they came in. We were strong females but the men were treated well at home.

My mum used to say to me if you were back home you would have servants and maids but other than that we came from what felt like an ordinary family. As immigrants we have strong values, work hard.

In time I headed off to lead a large team at the fourth-largest art collection in the United States, at the Philadelphia Museum of Art.

My job is about finding, influencing and communicating with growing audiences and increasing revenue. After six years I was headhunted to join the incredible team who were opening the Louvre in Abu Dhabi and I jumped at the opportunity to be part of history and help put that together. I really enjoyed my time there, even the strange work ethic and culture. My apartment was drop-dead gorgeous and the lifestyle quite opulent and surreal. It was so fascinating to be in this ancient land with its ancient stories.

Compared to the UK I felt less conscious about being black in Abu Dhabi and less conscious being a woman! It was a milestone project, historic and ambitious, all contributing to the 2030 vision of diversifying from oil for the nation. They hired and expected excellence.

There is a subtle way that institutional racism happens inside big UK organisations. Representation at middle management is fine but when you ask for promotion or wider opportunities to rise there is a block. At the Royal Academy this was my reality. A super-reinforced glass ceiling. I even had a senior colleague say to me, you already have a job, why do you want another one? How many times have you been in a board meeting or conference room and been the only black person in the room? That's pathetic in this day and age.

DEREK BLAKE
RESTAURATEUR

I find the newer generation of Caribbeans brought up in England do not have a strong identity of where they are from, or at least who they are and could be.

On the other hand, if I were to live a life thinking I am only a Jamaican, I would never be where I am today. There is so much potential to expand who you are.

And a lot of the kids here have never been to Jamaica but behave worse than ever. They always feel hard done by instead of being positive about what they want. Look at the other immigrants like the Indians and Polish; they are positive about what they can achieve here. For instance, when the Indians came here, I remember the talk, 'Let's go Paki bashing.' Of course I have never had any attitude towards anything, not defining myself as one thing or other people as one thing only. I have dreams and I give them a go.

I had success early when I bought a property in Muswell Hill and sold it for twice what I bought it for. I then got into the restaurant business and each one a success. I have had celebrities like Samuel Jackson, Spike Lee and Coldplay in here. Not bad for a dyslexic boy who used to herd goats back in Jamaica!

It's a shame. A lot of black people come into my Mango Room restaurant and say, 'There are no black people working!' That's because they all leave, they have an issue with serving people.

I literally go out in the street and ask if they want to work here because I employ people who walk in off the street anyway.

A lot of black people don't like the service industry. You don't see many black people working in restaurants, do you? They think it is degrading as people have always done that through slavery. Black Americans are different, they see themselves as American. We should call ourselves black English because it might make things better.

Jamaicans have Arawak Indian blood, Chinese blood too, many things going on. Then my kids are mixed between an English mother and an Anglo-Chinese mother. I don't even think about my kids' colour as it is all too mixed to say.

My philosophy is that I've always thought about moving my life forward and I try to bring this to my children.

A lot of black people don't like the service industry. You don't see many black people working in restaurants, do you? They think it is degrading as people have always done that through slavery. Black Americans are different, they see themselves as American. We should call ourselves black English because it might make things better.

GINA MATHARU
RESTAURATEUR

My uncle was a doctor in England and he brought Dad to London in 1960 and helped him get a job and accommodation in England. All seven of us lived with my uncle in a two-bedroom flat, which later included a new baby too. All of the five other kids slept in a bed together, but that was just how it was. As the eldest of my siblings, I had lots of jobs and responsibilities. I had to get up at 6am and make my uncle breakfast, then I'd go back to bed and get up again at 8am for school. Soon after this, the whole thing with Idi Amin happened and it wasn't safe for Asians to stay in Uganda, so my grandparents came to England too. My uncle bought a house in Birmingham for my grandparents and all of us. Dad had to go to London for work and eventually our family moved to Bethnal Green. When we were there, Mum worked as a machinist for the Jewish community and I looked after all the younger siblings. We managed to get an affordable house through that extra money. Then my aunt and uncle came to join us and I slept on the sofa. We all used the public baths at that time as it was cheaper.

My first marriage was physically abusive. One day, my husband grabbed me by the hair and pulled me all the way down the stairs because he said I had to put his dinner on the table for him. That shouldn't happen to anyone. During that time, I left twice with my three children and fled to my parents' home. However, they came to collect me and sent me back. They call it 'kismet': your fate, my mum said.

We lived only two doors down from his mother and I still felt trapped! Eventually in 1984 I had the strength to leave; I went to a refuge home and they were so good to me. We got a divorce and I ended up getting the house. Every time he came around I would have to call the police.

When I met my second husband John, I told him I had three conditions for our future together: one, no infidelity; two, my kids are THE most important thing; and three, don't ever lay a finger on me. We lived in a beautiful, small village on the west coast of Ireland. We had a gaggle of children and we worked hard to carve out a life for us all. We were very successful. I used the only skill I had: – cooking – to run an Indian café/restaurant along with a B&B business and we won loads of awards. John also had his own construction business. We had a lovely eight-bedroom/six-bathroom house with a pool overlooking the sea and we were very happy. Until I realised he had had a string of affairs.

I didn't realise, but I had a serious breakdown that year where I was on high doses of medication and I honestly don't remember any of it. I stayed in Ireland for a while, helping my eldest son and his wife to raise my grandson. When my youngest daughter, Serena, moved to Edinburgh, I decided to move here with her. I've found a life here working at a university café and the students treat me like a mother.

I still suffer from anxiety and I'm on medication to help with that. However, I've had a long-term dream to retire somewhere sunny by the sea. I haven't found the perfect place yet, but I will!

One day, he grabbed me by the hair and pulled me all the way down the stairs because he said I had to put his dinner on the table for him.

HOW TO THROW A BLUES PARTY

Since the 1980s we have witnessed the rise of the super clubs in the West End of London and beyond. We've been promised glitz and glamour, albeit along with snooty door staff and overpriced drinks! Clubbing is now such a democratic experience; access is granted to all who can pay and the tunes played are as eclectic as the crowd. It's not uncommon to see older people mingling with the youngsters – but are we really satisfied? Finding that homegrown feel in everything that we do nowadays needs nurturing and where better place to start than trying to capture that underground spirit – somewhere we can feel special? Here is a guide to throwing your very own retro blues dance. First thing you need is an abandoned building or a cleared-out front room.

AIN'T NOTHING GOING ON BUT THE RENT

Just to be clear, this party is being held because there is rent to be paid, unless someone is generously putting it on to celebrate an occasion – blues parties were first named 'rent' parties for this reason. Charge a quid at the door and run a cheap bar. Drinks and music must be familiar as this is a place for the familiar, the friendly, the antidote to the hardships going on 'out there'. Supply hard liquor like Wray and Nephew over-proof rum with coke, long-life beer, Cherry B and Babycham for the ladies who don't drink. Note: as some of these drinks are discontinued make up your own brand of similarly washing-up-liquid-flavoured drink and make your own labels to stick onto bottles.

BLUES-SPOT GRAM

A blues-spot-gram will be the centrepiece for smaller get-togethers – most people owned one. A beautifully crafted piece of furniture, often in teak, this drinks cabinet-come-music player with inbuilt speakers will sit pride of place in the living room – très chic!

SOUND BWOY

The Sound Bwoy is intrinsic to the blues dance and will provide the speakers, turntable and latest records. In the post-war era it was only white people who could afford to buy records but 'back a yard', where the Caribbean culture was emerging in Britain, Sound Bwoys would play the latest records on the street corner. The Caribbeans did not generally hold parties because folks did not have the space or money to and instead would gather to hear the latest tunes at the local sound systems such as Coxsone Sound. We can track the origins of the blues dance to the cultural ideas that merged at this time. The first idea being the use of sound systems 'back home' and secondly, the black American GIs who frequented Soho's jazz clubs just as they had done back in America, perpetuated the idea of club culture as a possibility for black people in Britain. These two cultural ideas were snatched up by entrepreneurial types, who would then hold their own blues dances in Britain. Black people were simply not made to feel comfortable in the West End clubs of London at the time, so the blues dances were the best social intercourse that Caribbeans had. Held on a Friday or Saturday, the disenfranchised 'owned' a place in a hostile land, if only for the night.

POLICE

If it is on the police agenda that week to spoil the party (since it is essentially an illegal rave), it's best to be prepared. If you are lucky, they have actually come to join in the good times so be sure to have a spare spliff to get them in the mood, that is, if the party girls don't get to them first.

MY GYAL DAT

There is etiquette to follow for the way in which guys and gals get together. The standard scene, of groups of boys on one end of the room proclaiming which girl/girls he likes at the other end of the room with 'my gyal dat', and facing the daunting death march across the room to introduce himself to a girl in front of all, is all too familiar. The custom to grab hold of a girl's wrist as she walks by is a lot less forgiving in case of rejection. It also helps in navigating the dark, jam-packed space.

DÉCOR
Black bin liners to adorn the windows will be atmospheric enough; without light you are transported into any time zone. Speaker boxes and the kitchen becomes a bar with a trestle table across the doorway.

WEAR A WATCH
When times are hard, value for money is key. Revelling can start at 8pm and go on till the sun comes up and beyond. Of course, after an all-nighter, disorientation will set in, so check your watch if you don't want to be late for work.

COME AS YOU ARE
Turning up from a work shift? No problem, take off your jacket and relax, just don't think you will be pulling that night, as your body odour reputation in the room will precede you. In fact come dressed for the next morning – that way you can stay all night and just go on to work.

MIND YOUR BACK
It is cold in England so keep the windows closed, if only to keep the ladies as scantily clad as possible. As it is often a necessity to stand up against the wall for lack of space or possibly because you are lost in music, gyrating with another soul, as the night wears on in this hot, dark, sweaty atmosphere, it can have you picking wallpaper off your back.

HOW TO THROW A BIG FAT INDIAN WEDDING

Indian weddings are nothing if not vibrant, colourful and loud! After centuries of perfecting their art in the subcontinent, all of the fun and grandeur has finally been brought to Britain's shores. The Indian wedding is as much an act of celebration and generosity as it is a symbol of status and pride. They are arguably the most elaborate in the world, so the first thing to do is get saving; excess is the only way and expense is rarely spared.

GOLDEN RULE NUMBER ONE
Indians love their food so one thing you can't do is scrimp on it. In fact, providing culinary delights for Indian weddings has become an industry in its own right in Britain. There's a huge array of catering companies to choose from and they all know how to feed at scale, from budget-tight to five-star extravagance.

PLUG IN THE EVEREADY BATTERY
Any Indian wedding will typically span the course of at least a week, so make sure you get your beauty sleep and keep the Red Bull on hand. Before the ceremony and main celebrations even get under way, there are a plethora of rituals and pre-party events that will require all your resources of energy and stamina. For Hindus, there's the Pithi and Mehndi. For Sikhs, there's the Maiyan, Chura, Sangeet and Jago.

DON'T LEAVE ANYONE OUT
It's essential not to offend any relatives, no matter how distant, so expect the guest list to be extensive. Even when you think you have invited only a family of four, it is entirely possible that they will decide, on the day, to bring their neighbour's family as well.

GIFTS ALL ROUND
If you are the eldest son or daughter of one of the wedding families, one of your many duties will be to run off to your best local Indian sweet shop to buy edible gifts for any relative or friend who happens to drop by the family home during the auspicious wedding period. These are gorgeously packaged treats in all manner of colours, laced with coconut, spices, condensed milk and lashings of honey. Enjoy!

SADDLE UP
For Sikhs and Hindus alike, it is traditional for the groom to arrive at the wedding mounted on a horse. Indeed, it is not uncommon to see particularly uncomfortable grooms, most of whom have never been horseback in their lives, straddling an equally wary-looking white steed through the urban streets on the special Indian wedding day. Basic equestrian lessons are therefore recommended for any Indian groom-to-be who is an unlikely contender for the Indian cavalry.

BLING GLORIOUS BLING
It's a well-known secret that most Indians stash their gold under the mattress. Those family heirlooms – elaborate 24-carat gold regalia of earrings, bracelets, necklaces, anklets and bindis – see the light of day when there is a knot to be tied. Just watch out, bridezilla, because those heavy earrings could increase your earlobes significantly after a week of celebrations.

BRING YOUR CASH
While many Indian couples have succumbed to the ever-practical department store gift list, the giving of cash is still commonplace. Particularly if you are a close relative of the bride or groom, you will normally be expected to cough up. Handfuls of cash are waved around the heads of the bride and groom before being placed in their laps. For Sikhs, it is viewed as good luck to give an amount ending in '1': £11, £21 or indeed £101.

BOLLYWOOD HERE WE COME!
The wedding reception is always of epic Bollywood proportions, complete with eardrum-busting

DJs, bhangra drums, celebrity-style video filming to capture every moment and perhaps even a professional dance performance. Get your hands in the air doing the 'light-bulb' move and those shoulders going to the beat.

WATCH UNCLE WITH THE WHISKY

There's always one, isn't there? Johnny Walker Black is the drink of prestige in India and a bottle or two will usually be placed on each guest table. The free-flowing spirits can, however, be too tempting for some and a very jolly uncle may just topple over on the dance floor before long.

EAT AND RUN

The later people stay, the better the wedding is judged to be. Therefore, a cunning plan for most Indian families is to draw out the food for as long as humanly possible. Once the guests know they have had the last of the dessert, they will be off. Indians don't hang around for anything else and clearly by this time everyone is exhausted anyway. Admit it: however much you love your son or daughter, it's finally over. Go home!

Marriage of Gurnek and Kylie Bains.

AFTERWORD

These stories have, we hope, brought to life the varied experiences of this pioneering generation. Contrasting themes emerge from these narratives. Just as people negotiated spirit-sapping challenges, hostility and rejection so also they found huge support, encouragement and eventual acceptance and success in their new homes. The multicultural battle over the decades was won more than it was lost.

But time does not stand still. The Windrush scandal and the rise of a narrower nationalism exemplified by Brexit have reaffirmed the age-old truth that battles in the field of race are never fully won. Things can always go backwards and time and history move in cycles. At times it has felt that the cosmopolitanism many have been enjoying in the last few decades of British history may have come and gone already.

The economic disparities in Britain have been sharply highlighted by the way Covid-19 has disproportionately hit black and Asian communities. BAME communities have been at the forefront as NHS, transport and shop workers during the crisis, and have borne the costs of this exposure. The graphic images that helped launch the Black Lives Matter movement tell us that all is still not well or settled in the experience of black and Asian people in this country or indeed elsewhere.

The recent vilification of the Duchess of Sussex, Meghan Markle, suggests that some parts of UK life are still not that easy for outsiders to enter. In the black community the pervasive belief is that she was punished by the media for her sheer audacity in 'spoiling the blood line'.

However, the technology of the internet and social media has empowered minority groups to find strength in numbers and to have their voice heard, achieving an interconnectedness that has not been possible before. The unfairness of history is also being exposed and the legacy of imperialism has finally been aired in a more truthful manner in this era of rapid news and memes. The horrors of slavery and history which dehumanised people of colour for economic gain, is now common knowledge. The foundations of the colonial empire were built on the myth that Commonwealth subjects were people to be patronised. This is now both exposed and challenged more openly.

A reaction to this ethnocentric backlash is taking place. Tens of thousands of protestors from all backgrounds have taken to the streets in the UK for the Black Lives Matter movement. The call for reparations and for school curriculum changes to share the full history of colonialism in the hope of stamping out the ignorance that gives rise to racial prejudice are now live issues.

But every reaction has a counterreaction. White nationalists have moved to protect statues and icons that reflect their view of history. The rise of extremism and destructive notions of nationalism and national identity, which do not grant acceptance to people who have a foreign accent or pigmented skin regardless of heritage, have gained new shoots from deep incendiary roots.

However, even for white nationalists there is a new complexity. When you stand outside your door clapping the NHS, you know a large proportion of it is composed of people from ethnic minorities. Football is another

Another world is not only possible, she is on her way. On a quiet day, I can hear her breathing. ARUNDHATI ROY

example of this complexity. Players of different complexions, often generations born here in the UK, are key contributors to the national team. If you are racist, how do you dismantle the complexities of this situation of love and of hate?

Despite the ups and downs, the overall situation is still moving in the right direction. It is clear Britain has become a melting pot of vibrant cultures, ideas, creativity and colour. In the last half-century, immigration has changed British society. Literally dozens of languages are spoken on the street. Fashion, art and dance is imbued with African, Caribbean and Indian aesthetics. From ethnically inspired modern art movements to the Caribbean beats that are the bedrock of pop music of all genres, the influence of migrant communities is tangible and profound.

The boundaries of nations are constructed, not fact. We as a society participate in the idea of who belongs and without new peoples creating new possibilities, we would be poorer as a society. How stagnant would a river be without the fresh tributaries incoming to refresh its flow? We hope the stories here will help people embrace new migrants with understanding and the sense that they too can help us move forward and continue to be the vibrant society that is needed to succeed in our ever complex and evolving world.

We also hope that these life stories help to maintain and deepen the progress that has been made by creating empathy and understanding across divides. Humanising the 'other' lies at the heart of building bridges. We also hope that the second- and third-generation children of the pioneers whom we have described are inspired by these accounts and continue the journey begun by their forebears, deepening both their connection with their past and striving for ever greater success within British society.

OVERLEAF Street celebration during the Silver Jubilee of Queen Elizabeth II, London, 1977.

Afterword 203

INDEX

Page references in *italics* indicate images.

A

Abbott, Diane 64
Abisinde (community initiative housing trust) 103
Adebambo, Jean 153
Adu, Ralph *148*, 149, 150, *150*, *151*
African Caribbean Mental Health Service 103
All Saints Road, Notting Hill 74, 77, *77*, 128, *128*, 129, 157, 158, *158*
Ashwood-Garvey, Amy 33

B

Bailey-Smith, Yvonne *20*, 21, *22–3*, 24, 37, 167, *167*
Bains, Piara Singh *7*, 98, *98*, 99–100, *100*, 101, *101*, 145
Bains, Swarn Kaur *26*, 27–8, *28*, 29, *29*
Band Nectar 171
BBC 53, 95, 96, 160, 181, 185, 191
Beaton, Norman 133
Bedako, Stirling 107
Berman, Ed 133
Bhattacharya, Ramen 95
Bird, John 95
Black Lives Matter movement 200
Black Market Records 161
Black Power 33, 107, 133–4, 166
Black Theatre Workshop 180
Blackwell, Chris 75
Blair, Tony 95
Blake, Derek *192*, 193
blues dance/blues party 74, 111, 141, 143, 145, 153, 157; how to throw a 196–7, *197*
Blues-spot gram 143, 153, 196
BNP (British National Party) 61, 63, *63*
Bogle, Paul 93
Bradford 30, *30*, 34, 40, *40*, 48, 50, 57; riots/protest (2001) 67
Brexit 11, 18, 200
Brick Lane, London 117, *118–19*
British Empire 66, 90, 175, 185, 200
British Nationality Act (1948) 185
British Transport Films 121

Brixton, London *68–9*, 69, 103, 149, 153, 171; riots (1981) 64, *64–5*, 67, 153
Broadwater Farm riots, London (1985) 67
Bullers foundry, Sandwell 36, *36*

C

Cameron, Earl 179
Careem, Nic *94*, 95–7, *96*, *97*
Carmichael, Peter 107
Carmichael, Stokely 133
Central St Martins, London 122
Chaggar, Gurdip Singh 61, 63, *63*
churches 33, 62, 68, *68–9*, 69, *70–1*, 114, *115*, 143, 144, 145, *145*, 187, 189
cinema 57, 133, *142*, 143–4, *154*, 155, 175
class system 33, 40, 57, 67, 83, 107, 134, 179, 180–1, 238
Cleopatra (film) 175
club culture 143, 144, 194
Cochrane, Kelso 73
Colonial House hostel, Kensington 18, *19*, 67
Coloured People's Progressive Association 62
Commonwealth 61, 90, *90–1*, 113, 165, 185, 200
Conservative Party 95, 96, 97, *97*, 128
convenience stores/corner shops 39, 40, 111, 116, 117, *117*, *118–19*, 155, 200
Count Suckle 73, 153
Covid-19 pandemic, BAME communities and 11, 42, 116, 200
Critchlow, Frank 128, 157
Cry Freedom (film) 180
curry 56, *56*, 61, 116, 165

D

Daddy Vego *92*, 93, *93*
Dass, Dharam *168*, 169
Devine, George 179
Dhir, Vijay *6*, *110*, 111, *120*, 121–3, *122*, *123*, *124*, *125*
DJ culture 143, 144, 153, 161, 183
Duke Vin 73, 127, 153

E

Ealing, London 61, 62
Eastern European migrants 11, 18
EDL (English Defence League) 61, 63, *63*
Edwards, Beresford 104
Edwards, Elouise *102*, 103–4, *104*, *105*, 112
Elizabeth, Queen Mother 122, 123, *123*
Elizabeth II, Queen 107, 175, 187; Silver Jubilee (1977) 201, *202–3*
EpiTombe 180
Equity (actors' union) 179, 180, 181
Evening Standard 181, 185

F

Fagan, Bevan 'Bagga' 153
Fame, Georgie 73, 127
First World War (1914–18) 90
football 200–1
Four Aces Club, Dalston Lane, London 129, *130–1*
Francis, Jenni 42, *190*, 191
Freitas, Michael de 133

G

gang warfare 62
Garvey, Marcus 33, 93
Ghana 33, 137, 149, 179, 181
Gordon, Aloysius 'Lucky' 19, 67, *72*, 73–5, *74*, *75*, *76*, 77
Greater London Council (GLC) 122, 179
Green Banana Theatre 133
Gregory, Dick 133
Guru Granth Sahib *58*, 59
Guyana 103–4

H

Handsworth riots (1981) 67
Hans Crescent, Knightsbridge 179
Harlem Renaissance 133
Harrison, George 155
Hashmi, Shazardi 57
Heathrow Airport *14*, 21, 31, 34, 42, 43, *43*
Henderson, Russell 166, *166*, *170*, 171, 172, *172*, *173*
Home Office *13*, 64, *64*, 165
home ownership 111–13

Howe, Darcus 107, 133–4
Hughes, Langston 133
Hull 79
Human Rights Coalition 169

I
ICA [Institute of Contemporary Arts] 133
Ilford Odeon, London 144
India 11, 27, 28, 31, 39, 40, 47, 53, 54, 56, *56*, 57, 61, 64, 67, 89, 90, 98, 99–100, 101, 111, 112, 116, 117, 121, 143, 144, 145, 155, 165, 167, 169, 195, 198, 199, 201
Indian restaurants 56, *56*, 165
Indian wedding, how to throw a big fat 198–9, *199*
Indian Workers' Association 61
Island Records 73, 75

J
Jallianwala Bagh massacre, Golden Temple, Amritsar (1919) 90
Jamaica 21, 45, 74, 75, 81, 89, 90, 93, 127, 137, 143, 152, 153, 157, 179, 189, 193
Jamaican Diaspora UK 81
Janner, Greville 169
Jarvis, Basil 93
jazz dancing 144, *144*
Jean-Marie, Kenneth 82, *82*, 83

K
Kalipha, Stefan *106*, 107, *107*
Keeler, Christine 73, 74, 75, 77, 129
Kenya 14, 35, 169
Kirpal, Swarn *52*, 53, 54, *54*, 55, *55*, 185
Kiss FM 161
knife crime 62
Knight, Beverly 90, 187, 188, 189
Kray Twins 73

L
Labour Party 47, 95, 97, 169
Ladbroke Grove, London 33, 67, 73, *88*, 89, 111, 127, *136*, 137, 158, *158*, 159, *159*, 171
Laslett, Ronnie 171
Leamington 47
Leslie, Gloria *80*, 81, *81*
Liberty Cinema, Southall *154*
Licorish, Darance 67, 93, 127–8
Lindon, John 107

Littlewood, Joan 179
Lord Cloak 127
lovers rock 153
Lumumba ('Mumba'), Patrice 179
Luther King Jr., Martin 68
Lynch, Josette 66, 68

M
Mahmood, Sultan 34, 40
Mahoney, Louis *178*, 179–81, *180*, *181*
Mangrove, All Saints Road 73–4, 77, *77*, 129, 157
March for Unity, Southall (1976) 62
Matharu, Gina, 194, 195
Matthews, Charlie 128
Matura, Mustapha *132*, 133, 134, *135*
May, Theresa 185
Metro, The, Ladbroke Grove 127
Michael X 107
Milner-Brown, Mae 32, *32*, 33, 146
Milner-Brown, Val *6*, *136*, 137, 138, *138*, 139, *139*
Minshall, Peter 163
Mosley, Oswald 67
Moss Side, Manchester 66, 104, *108*, 112; riots (1981) 67
'my gyal dat' 196–7

N
Nana Bonsu Library 104
National Front 61, *110*, 111, 123, *124*, *125*, 149
nationalism 200
NHS (National Health Service) 11, 40, 42, 62, 90, 200
night shifts 31, 39, 47, 53, 121
'No blacks, No Irish, No dogs' signs 23, *25*, 112
North Kensington Amenity Trust 67
Notting Hill, London *60*, 61, 66, *66*, 67, 73, 74, 77, *77*, 107, 112, 128, *128*, *129*, 153, 157, *162*, *163*, 166, *166*, 167, *167*, 171; Carnival *60*, 61, 66, *66*, 67, 93, 107, 153, *162*, 166, *166*, 171, 172, *172*; riots (1958) 67, 73
nurses 21, 40, *40*, 42, 80, 81, *81*, *186*, 187, *188*, 189, *189*
Nuttall, Dick 138, *138*

O
Oldham 67
Ové, Horace 107, 133, *174*, 175, 176, *176*, 177

P
Paddington Station, London *16*, 17, *120*, 121
'partners', Caribbean practice known as 112
Patel, Mahesh 31, 38
Pearson, Sheron 152, *152*, 153, 183
Peckham Bus Garage, London 40, *41*
People's Sound, Notting Hill 93, *93*
Performers Against Racism referendum 181
Philip, 'Gus' Osmond 67, *88*, 89, 93, *93*, *156*, 157, 158, *158*, 159, *159*, 160, *160*, 161, *161*, *184*, 185
Philips, Trevor 95
pirate radio 159, 160, *160*, 161
Police Authority 47
police prejudice 67, 73, 93, 103, 123, 128, 157, 161, 166, 179, 196
Pool of London *18*
Post Office 45, 47, 49, *49*, 53, 54, 99, 191
Powell, Enoch 63, *63*, 169
Pratt, Mary Louise 116
Pressure (first UK black feature film) 175, *176*
pubs 180–1
Punjab, India 27, 28, 47, 54, 64, 99, 101, 111, 121, 169

Q
Quadras, Francis 2, 35, *35*
Quarshie, Hugh 181

R
Racial Adjustment Action Society 62
racism 18, 21, 39, 42, 43, 54, 57, 61, 63, *63*, 64, *64*, 67, 68, 90, 95, 116, 121, 128, 166, 169, 171, 176, 181, 189, 191, 200, 201
Radio Caroline 161
railway workers 47, *82*, 83, 98, *98*, 99, *120*, 121–3, *122*, *123*, 165
Reece, Rowland 133
regeneration and gentrification projects, council 113, *113*
reggae culture 93, *93*, 153, 157, 159, 161, 166
Repton Foundry 48, *48*
riots 62, 63, *63*, 64, *64*–5, 67, 73, 153
rogue landlords 67
'Rooms to Let – No Coloured Men' signs 25, *25*
Rosen & Co. 57

Royal Academy of Arts, London 191
Royal Commission 122
Royal Court Theatre, London 133, 179
Roy, Arundhati 201

S
Scandal (film) 73
Scarman Report 67
Schloss, Eva 95
seaside, trips to the 33, 100, 146, *146*, *147*
Secker, Johnny 179
Second World War (1939–45) 90, 90–1, 185
Sehgal, Satish and Maya 155
Selasi, Taiye 15
Shafi, The, Gerrard Street 56, *56*
Sharma, Kamala 79
shebeens 73, 143, 157
shift work 31, 36, *36*, 39, 42, 47, 53, 121, 145
Sikhs 18, 27, 47, 61, 63, 64, *64*, 89, 90, 98, 99, 198
Singh, Mota 7, 46, *46*, 47, 48
Smith, Deloris 7, 31, 42, 43, 90, *186*, 187, 188, *188*, 189, *189*
Smithfield Market, London 64, *64*
Smith, Zadie 7, 21, 167, *167*
Soca Gakkai 107
Soho, London 12, *12*, 196

Sound Bwoy 196
sound systems 143, 153, 157, 196
South Africa 33, 180, 181
Southall Carnival (1977) 62, *63*
Southall, London 28, 28, 29, *29*, *49*, 61, 62, *62*, 63, *63*, 64, *64*, 90, 112, 115, *115*, 121, *154*, 167, *167*
Southey, Percy 61
Soyinka, Wole 179
Springfield, Dusty 33
St Bart's Hospital, London 21
steel bands 107, 171
Stevenson's Box Works 103
St Lucia 83
St Pancras Station, London 83
Stratford East Theatre, London 179
Studio One label 143
Sussex, Meghan Markle, Duchess of 200
Sweeny, Frank 127

T
Tabernacle, Ladbroke Grove 127, 159, *159*
Taj Stores, Brick Lane 117, *118–19*
teachers 27, 33, 53, 68, 99, 127, 128, 179
Tella, Sylvia 161
textile factories *30*, 31, 40, *41*, 50, *51*
theatre 133–4, 179, 180
Theatre Machine 179

Toxteth riots (1981) 67
Trinidad 107, *132*, 133, 166, 171, 175, 189
TSPO (Trinidad Steel Percussion Orchestra) 107
Turner, Errol *44*, 45
12 Bar Club, London 148, 149, 150, *150*, *151*

U
Uddin, Komor 117, *118–19*
Uganda 43, *43*, 79, 155, 169, 195

W
Ward, Stephen 74
Watson, Errol 73
weather 17, 21, 27, 31, 99, 107, 171
weddings 155, 198–9
West End, London *4–5*, 93, 127, 143, 171, 179, 196
Wilkinson, Sheila Scott 107
Windrush 66, *66*, 113, 180, 185; scandal 11, 200
Wolverhampton 66, *66*, *129*, *140*, 169

Y
Young, Dorothy 40, *40*, 68, 109, 112, *112*, 141, 145, *145*

ACKNOWLEDGEMENTS

Gurnek and Bryony would first like to pay their respects to their parents, the inspiration for this book. We are indebted to all the wonderful folk who let us into their homes and gave us their time and stories. We thank Dr Ekua McMorris and Maya Bewick, who took many of the photographs, and to Vanley Burke and David Corio for agreeing to let us use some of their incredible work. We are thankful to all the photographers who have supplied photos in archives that we have been able to share and particularly to Ealing Central Library for their donation.

We are also indebted to Rajinder Bains, Kiran Kotega, and Satinder Bains who helped us with some of the interviews and with collecting a number of the images. We also want to thank Profile Books for their professionalism and support. A big thank you also goes to the think tank, Global Future, who supported the project both financially and in spirit. Anita Kirpal, in particular, provided great support.

Bryony would also like to thank her husband Paul and her family for standing by and supporting this project and to her sister Lola for having the foresight, age 10, to save the family photos lying around the house and keep in an album.

Gurnek, Bryony and Kylie

PHOTO CREDITS

t = top, t/l = top left, t/r = top right, m = middle, b = bottom, b/l = bottom left, b/r = bottom right

Photographs courtesy of the following contributors:
2 © Vanley Burke
4–5 © Shawshots/Alamy Stock Photo
6 *t* Dorothy Young, *b/l* Valerie Milner-Brown, *b/r* Swarn Kaur Bains
7 *t/l* Mota Singh, *t/r* Yvonne Bailey-Smith, *b/r* Piara Singh Bains, *b/r* Mota Singh
9 *t/l* Swarn Bains, *t/r* Mae Milner-Brown, *b/l*, left to right Milner-Brown sisters (Valerie and Louise), *b/r* mother Dorcus, Louise
10 Zane Lee
12 © Bert Hardy/*Picture Post*/Hulton Archive/Getty Images
13 please ignore this one
14 © Keystone/Getty Images
16 © Edward Miller/Keystone/Getty Images
18–9 © Bert Hardy/*Picture Post*/Hulton Archive/Getty Images
20, 22–3 © Dr Ekua McMorris
24 Yvonne Bailey-Smith
25 © Keystone Features/Getty Images
26 Swarn Kaur Bains
28 © Ealing Central Library
29 *t* Swarn Kaur Bains, *b* © Ealing Central Library
30 © Central Press/Getty Images
31 © *Evening Standard*/Getty Images
32 Mae Milner-Brown
34 © Fox Photos/Getty Images
35 © Central Press/Getty Images
36 © Peter Marlow/Magnum
38 © Ian Berry/Magnum
40 *t* A. Abbas/Magnum, *m*, *b* Dorothy Young
41 © Central Press/Hulton Archive/Getty Images
42–3 © David Hurn/Magnum
44 © Dr Ekua McMorris
46 Mota Singh
48 *t* © Terence Spencer/The LIFE Picture Collection via Getty Images,
b © Val Doone/Getty Images
49 © Ealing Central Library
51 © A. Abbas/Magnum
52, 54–5 Swarn Kirpal
56 © Thurston Hopkins/Picture Post/Hulton Archive/Getty Images
58 © Vanley Burke
60 © Chris Steele-Perkins/Magnum
62–5 © Ealing Central Library
66 *t* © Chris Steele-Perkins/Magnum, *b* © Martin Parr/Magnum
68–9 © Chris Steele-Perkins/Magnum
70–1 © Vanley Burke
72 © Malindine, Bill/Mirrorpix/Mirrorpix via Getty Images
74–5 Aloysius 'Lucky' Gordon
76–7 © Malindine, Bill/Mirrorpix/Mirrorpix via Getty Images
78 © Peter Marlow/Magnum
80 © Maya Bewick
81 Dorothy Young
82 *t/l*, *t/r* © Kenneth Jean-Marie, *b* © Ian Berry/Magnum
84–5 © Ian Berry/Magnum
86, 88 © Dr Ekua McMorris
91 © Iconographic Archive/Alamy Stock Photo
92–3 © Dr Ekua McMorris
94, 96 Nic Careem
97 © Peter Marlow/Magnum
98, 100–1 Piara Singh Bains
102, 104–5 © Dr Ekua McMorris
106 © Maya Bewick
107 © Stefan Kalipha
108 © Martin Parr/Magnum
110 Vijay Dhir
112 Dorothy Young
113 © Charlie Phillips/Hulton Archive/Getty Images
114 © Chris Steele-Perkins/Magnum
115 © Ealing Central Library
117 © Thurston Hopkins/*Picture Post*/Hulton Archive/Getty Images
118–9 © Michael Fresco/*Evening Standard*/Hulton Archive/Getty Images
120 © Dr Ekua McMorris
122–5 Vijay Dhir
126 © Sergio Larrain/Magnum
128 © Dr Ekua McMorris
129 © Chris Steele-Perkins/Magnum
130–1 © David Corio
132, 135–6 © Dr Ekua McMorris
138 *b/l* © Patrick Reddin, *b/r* © Valerie Milner-Brown
139 Valerie Milner-Brown
140 © Chris Steele-Perkins/Magnum Photos
142 © *Evening Standard*/Getty Images
144 © Bert Hardy/*Picture Post*/Hulton Archive/Getty Images
145 Dorothy Young
146 © Vanley Burke
147 © David Hurn/Magnum
148, 150–1 © Maya Bewick
152 © Sheron Pearson
154 © Ealing Central Library
156, 158–61 © Dr Ekua McMorris
162 © Ian Berry/Magnum
164 © Vanley Burke
166 © Fred Mott/*Evening Standard*/Hulton Archive/Getty Images
167 *t* © Ealing Central Library, *b* Yvonne Bailey-Smith
168 Dharam Dass
170, 172–4, 176–8, 180–1, 184, 186, 188–9, 192 © Dr Ekua McMorris
182 © Ekua McMorris
190 Jenni Francis
194 Gina Matharu
199 Gurnek and Kylie
202–3 © Chris Steele-Perkins/Magnum

Front cover image
Schoolchildren, Salford, 1977
Rod Varley / Alamy Stock Photo

Back cover image
© Central Press/Getty Images

Gurnek Bains

Gurnek Bains came over to Britain at the age of six from the Punjab in India. He is a psychologist by background and Managing Partner of the leadership consulting firm Global Future. He is also CEO of Global Future a think-tank devoted to flying the flag for an open and inclusive world. Gurnek is also on the board of Intertek PLC as well as Chair of Akram Khan, a leading dance company championing a uniquely British-Asian art form.

Kylie Bains

Kylie came to England from Australia in 1991 and has two mixed-race children of Indian-Australian descent. She is passionate about embracing individual and cultural diversity, which led to her co-founding the Global Future think-tank and leadership consultancy. She is a business psychologist, key author of *Meaning Inc: The Blueprint for Business Success in the 21st Century* and was previously a director of YSC, a global leadership consultancy.

PROFILE EDITIONS

First published in Great Britain in 2020 by Profile Editions, an imprint of Profile Books Ltd
29 Cloth Fair,
London EC1A 7JQ
www.profileeditions.com

Copyright © Global Future CIC, 2020

Printed and bound in Italy by Lego srl.

All rights reserved. Without limiting the rights under copyright reserved above, no part of this publication may be reproduced, stored or introduced into a retrieval system, or transmitted, in any form and by any means (electronic, mechanical, photocopying, recording or otherwise) without the prior written permission of both the copyright owner and the publisher of this book.

A CIP catalogue record for this book is available from the British Library.

ISBN 9781788167963

Design concept:
Bryony Heard

Cover design and layout:
Caroline Clark

Bryony Heard

Bryony has worked in the arts and entertainment industry for over 20 years. She began her career as a backing singer for David Bowie and other artists, as well as writing songs for films and developing artists. She has a degree in theatrical costume and set design from the Royal Central School of Speech and Drama. More recently Bryony has been an archivist for the *Always Print the Myth* exhibition at the V&A. She is an advisor to the Global Future Arts and Culture.

Global Future is a think tank working across politics, business and the arts to champion openness and inclusion.